THE
GARDEN
OF MEANING

by

SHAYKH FADHLALLA HAERI

...lications

REVIEWS FOR THE GARDEN OF MEANING

The Garden of Meaning is about two gardens, one visible and fragrant, the other less visible but eternal. The beauty and harmony of both gardens are exposited in this magisterial volume, linking outer to inner, physics to metaphysics, self to cosmos. It is an invitation to all seekers, whatever their background, age or station, with peace the only goal and growth the only certainty.

Bruce B. Lawrence. Marcus Family Humanities Professor of Religion Emeritus, Duke University. Latest Book: The Koran in English - A Biography

Shaykh Fadhlalla Haeri has given us a contemporary *Garden of Meaning*, a work that not so much looks back on mystical classics as to recreate them here and now, in today's language. Sufis describe God as the *Haqq*, the Real, the Reality, and the Truth. Haeri's book is a profound meditation on this Haqq as our origin, our path, and our destination. We are immersed in the Ocean of the Real, even as we desperately seek the Truth. We are the fish in the ocean, wondering where the water is. Haeri's book is a beautiful awakening to that ocean in which we already are, from which we have never been apart.

Omid Safi, Professor of Islamic Studies, Duke University. Author: Radical Love: Teachings from the Islamic Mystical Tradition.

In this luminous book Shaykh Fadhlalla Haeri has gifted his readers with profound existential and ethical insights from the Sufi tradition presented with sharp lucidity and clarity. Embracing all of existence, this book is a generous rendering of core Sufi teachings that resonate at an inclusive and universal spiritual register, integrating seamlessly knowledge from a range of disciplines. A polish for the heart, Shaykh Haeri points us to the radical freedom, capacity and responsibility each human life carries for purifying him or herself – and a beautiful reminder of the bountiful inner resources available to do so. A spiritual primer for our times, this book urges us to see with both eyes, to be responsive to the changing dynamic social realities while nourishing the heart from the eternal zone of the Divine One.

Sa'diyya Shaikh, Associate Professor, University of Cape Town. Author: Sufi Narratives of Intimacy, Ibn Arabi, Gender and Sexuality.

Acknowledgements

Several people have assisted with this book. Shameen Yacoob has been the main help throughout and Muneera Haeri's contribution in editing and supervision has been indispensible. Thanks to Zaheer Cassim and Yunus Ismail for their loyal support and to all those who reviewed the book.

Distributed and Published by Zahra Publications
P O Box 50764
Wierda Park 0149
Centurion
South Africa
www.sfhfoundation.com
www.zahrapublications.com
© 2018 Shaykh Fadhlalla Haeri

Typeset in South Africa by Mizpah Marketing Concepts
Cover Painting by Shaykh Fadhlalla Haeri
Cover Design by Mariska Botes
ISBN 978-1-919826-56-1

TABLE OF CONTENTS

Preface

The 15th century mystic poet Kabir said, *"It is good knowing that glasses are to drink from, the bad thing is not knowing what thirst is for."* The philosopher can end up becoming infatuated with the glass, the religionist with putting it on an altar, or worshipping the one who carried the glass.

In this book, Shaykh Fadhlalla Haeri shows us not only what thirst is for, but the origin of and reason for the thirst itself.

Using the metaphor of life as a *garden of meaning*, Shaykh Fadhlalla shows us that, approached with a cultivator's eye, every experience, longing and desire that we have—as well as every process, natural and artificial, practical or virtual, that we find within or around us—grow toward one purpose.

"Your life's journey is like a walk in a sacred park, where every grass and flower and tree has its own story and cycle of beginnings and ends."

The words *meaning* and *purpose* are misleading here. As the author shows us, the experience we are all looking for in life lies beyond the wisdom that can be expressed in thoughts or words. So the use of words in the book has the subtle effect of offering ideas with one hand while removing even more with the other, a bit like setting a table laid with finely-crafted cutlery and glasses and then whisking away, not only the table cloth underneath them, but also the table itself. As a zen koan intimates, the words are mere fingers pointing to the moon.

As in his earlier book, *Spectrum of Reality*, Shaykh Fadhlalla avoids the use of religious, mystical or metaphysical terminology. Due to his background in science, and his interest in relating its latest discoveries to the innate processes of self-discovery, readers of any or no spiritual background can benefit. At the same time, those familiar with the Shaykh's beautiful commentaries on the Qur'an will find that the present book deepens their understanding even more. Nonetheless, some readers may be shocked, as he challenges us to release cherished conceptions that veil us from what is really going on:

"Through meditation or psychotropic drugs many people experience boundless consciousness or a touch of infinitude. Religious people often refer to it in religious terms, with a certain amount of reverential confusion, as sacredness, divine precinct, holy spot or bliss. There is usually an insinuation that a teacher, master or guru, dead or alive, can give it to you. The gullibility of humans is such that we really do think that someway, somehow, somebody can take you out of the misery of yourself."

"The gift of life within everyone is like a well that continuously provides quality water and sustenance. With the growth of conditioned consciousness and our minds, habits and accumulated memories, this well gets filled up with debris and junk that only you know the extent and density of it. For quality life, you have to clear out the junk from your well. Nobody else can do it for you."

The overall effect of the book builds slowly, so I would recommend taking it slowly, perhaps a chapter a day upon arising or retiring. The best medicines release gradually, over time, and then disappear from the system completely without unwanted side effects, leaving one more healthy than before. To the extent that any book of wisdom can do the same, this one does, leaving the reader more human than before, in touch with both soul and self in a transformed way.

Neil Douglas-Klotz

(Saadi Shakur Chishti)

April 2018

Fife, Scotland

INTRODUCTION

Our natural love of gardens has many facets which include shape, size, colours, textures, smell, touch and other feelings. We always seek harmony and connectedness and our sensory stimulations send a message of acceptance or rejection. When our body and mind are at ease we move towards higher consciousness and transcend the limitations of our mind. Our love of the perfect garden is thus a representation of our passion to experience cosmic perfection.

I grew up in an environment where visiting beautiful gardens and reading poetry describing heavenly gardens were central to the culture. Shabistari's *Secret Rose Garden* was prominent among such renderings. After various attempts to improve on the translation of his writings I had a dream of Shabistari advising me to write what is appropriate for the time and world I was living in, rather than looking at past creatively-inspired works.

There are two gardens for reflective people. One is temporary and ever changing, while the other relates to deep meaning and insights. *The Garden of Meaning* touches both zones — the sensory garden as well as inner joy. Outer gardens and our love of beauty and harmony are doorways to the inner state of the perfect spirit within, which reflects the cosmic divine source.

From this one source and essence multiple universes and existences appear and change in dynamic flux. Whatever our senses discern emanates from a source which asserts itself in numerous ways and most prominently through the natural search and investigation that is in our human nature. Every form has a meaning that influences our perception of it. All human experiences connect physical, chemical and biological states with higher consciousness and ultimately with the unifying cosmic Reality or singularity. The human desire to explore forms and meanings is like climbing higher along the ladder of consciousness. The supreme or divine Reality is the ultimate meaning behind what exists in the universe, as such it permeates all that is known and unknown.

All human experience is thus an attempt to help us rise in consciousness from the limitations of conditioned consciousness to its boundless, infinite origin. The ultimate challenge is to realise that personal life is inseparable from perpetual cosmic life. This realisation is the root of durable contentment and happiness, for the purpose, meaning and direction of whatever there is in the universe is to be at one with the One and only One.

TO BEGIN

Whatever we experience

in life has a beginning.

Human existence is

within space-time,

therefore there are

endless beginnings

and ends strung along

a continuity that is

perpetual.

REALITY AND TRUTH

All experiential realities are transitory and short-lived, yet we seek that which endures and is considered to be true or real. We desire connections that are naturally sustainable and continuous. We even try to convince ourselves of experiencing truth. We are desperate for Truth! We are obsessed with truth and yet constantly distracted from it. Truth is with you whoever and wherever you are, and its light illuminates the universe in numerous ways. Truth permeates all and there is no possible turning away from it. Its intensity and clarity varies in accordance with our focus and attention.

Falsehood, doubts and uncertainty permeate the zone of duality and the confines of space-time. Truth itself is ever in unity but our world of sensory experiences appears as duality whilst we evolve in consciousness towards higher consciousness and the origin of oneness. Truth has no specific path to it, but the idea of path and direction emanate from it. When all questions end, truth shines. Every flicker of truth or what appears as real, is a minor reflection of the Real. Truth originates from beyond the limitations of space or time but also permeates the multiverse.

All things that exist are unsustainable and are like all shadows, short or long lived within space. Truth is constant and eternal, everything emanates from It, is sustained by It and returns to It. Truth is the essence of the universe, which is energised by varying levels of intensity and strength of truth. That is why Truth itself is diluted and filtered for us so as to enable us to survive our earthly illusion of separation and independence.

Life on earth in a physical sense arose after the intensity of the light and the heat of the sun was minimised by the atmosphere. In the same way, the power of cosmic Light and divine Power had to be filtered and reduced before it could bring sentiency and consciousness to atoms and molecules. Truth and Reality are at the source and essence of existence and creation, permeating all to varying degrees of intensity. Since our origin is that zone, we are obsessed with what we consider to be true or real. The human soul carries the imprint of truth and that is the source of our obsession and drive.

Beginning And End

Life is endless, but personal experience of it has a beginning and an end, which our relentless pursuits signify and acknowledge. All human quests end when our consciousness transcends body and mind limitations whilst alive or upon death. The end is the same as its birth, since both emerged from boundless timelessness. We live within the limitations of space-time, which is reinforced by personal and collective experiences. We also perceive the universe as having a beginning and an end. Scientific pursuit seeks the origin and the limit of the universe. The nuclear micro world is one side that doesn't end, the other is astrophysics and what is colossal and beyond limits. Quests to understand the inner world and the nature of the smallest entities are balanced by our quest for the big world and the nature of the universe and cosmos. The more we discover the more there is. Reality is boundless and our life is a limited sample of this reality.

Attempts to solve the mystery of existence tackle countless related issues, except the mystery itself. Life is a perpetual mystery and puzzle, and all outer searches are a distraction from awakening to the truth that transcends this mystery. Our material composition and mental identity relate to metaphysical origin. Whatever we discern physically is a manifestation of a subtle realm of energy that itself has emerged from a subtler origin. The human mind connects physics with metaphysics. The boundless cosmic grace and subtle realities connect with ever-changing local situations through the faculty of the mind and the self. Our mind and thoughts are earthly. Our insights and lights of the soul are heavenly. The two realms define our humanity and divinity. All dualities are from one origin!

It is in our nature to start something new and it is also in our nature to conclude and bring it to an end. The hamster in us is perpetually on that wheel in the cage of space-time, whilst yearning for that which is beyond the cage's boundaries, and that is the nature of our own soul or spirit. Who is it that is looking for what? Differentiation will only come to rest at oneness. Awakening implies accepting the temporary experience of dualities and entities, whilst knowing that Truth transcends all and is the cause of all that moves and changes. One's soul knows the Ever-Constant, and it is our soul that we yearn for!

SPACE — TIME

Whatever exists interconnects, relates and communicates through different channels within space-time. The entire universe is held together by vibrations that cause stimulation and response. Our five senses scan a wide range of mediums of connection. Hearing is a vibration that comes to us via the air medium. Sight relates to photons, each one of which is a particle as well as a wave function. A touch is a direct interpretation of what is being touched through the nerves. Thousands of olfactory receptors convey to us the smell that enhances the taste of what we eat.

Our sensory faculties comprise numerous and varied levels and layers, each with their own system of laws, regulations, interactions, and evolutionary changes. All human experiences are like traces made in time within frames of space. So long as we experience life through our sensory faculties we are confined to conditioned consciousness and the limitations of space-time.

The point of conception in the womb is the beginning of an evolutionary process leading ultimately to the human reality, which experiences space-time, and lights and energies that stretch beyond space-time. These lights are boundless and emanate from the cosmic origin beyond our comprehension. The human soul or spirit is like a holographic representation of the cosmic spirit and the life force which we experience and wonder about its purpose and direction. The soul's earthly journey will carry traces of experiences and values that will be shed after death. Our love to connect and communicate simply reflects the cosmic connection of our own soul and its divine origin. We investigate and ponder upon the nature of time and its multifaceted dimensions.

We do not know what time is and how it gives rise to the experience of movement and change. Space-time is very relative and as such we can imagine both timelessness and infinite space. Space-time emanates from a zone of consciousness that is not bound by any time or any space and the human soul carries that imprint and for that reason we can never be content in any of the limitations of space-time.

LIGHT AND DARKNESS

Beginnings and ends merge together into existence and return together inseparably. So too with light and darkness. Between the primal cosmic Light and visible light lies countless levels and zones, like the electromagnetic field spanning a vast array of frequencies. We naturally seek a light that gives us a greater clarity and illumination, yet it is always shadows and darkness that lead us to where light is more effulgent. It is the contrast between light and shadow, ignorance and knowledge that enables us to seek greater light.

We naturally seek ways out of limitations and confinement of space-time, preferring ease and familiarity. Life's journey is like groping in shadows and uncertainties in order to relate, connect and understand. Movement is perceived through our senses when different snapshots are strung together at a speed of about 20 frames a second — a wonderful play of lights, shadows and matter. Most of our experiences vary in clarity, understanding and reliability. Mind and intellect provide rationality, objectivity and a high sense of intelligence. This shared conditioned consciousness enables us to understand the concept of normality, sanity, a healthy mind and well-being.

The move to the energy field of aspiring to becoming a contented being is like coming out of darkness into the light. Body and mind belong to the cave of limitations, and the self — which is only the shadow of the soul — yearns for its origin beyond dark and light. That is light of grace, not visible light. A black hole where all personal consciousness ends and personal life merges back with its origin of cosmic mystery. Each moment vanishes into the black hole for the next instant to appear. Endless light and darkness emanate from cosmic oneness, the mystery that encompasses all.

All stars within a galaxy revolve around a black hole and our experience of space-time is due to our state of experiencing the constantly vanishing moment and the illusion of separation and need to preserve personal life! Time is actually timeless and so is the divine light without shadows. This experience of the movement of time, like every moment or instant, is at the event horizon of falling into the black hole and disappearing. The next moment follows on and on, appearing from nowhere and disappearing into oblivion.

FORM AND MEANING

The planet is composed of matter energised by numerous entities and strands of energy and radiations. Our visible and tangible world is celestial in origin and terrestrial in form and appearance.

The human being has an earthly frame with a heavenly meaning, drive and purpose. We experience diverse manifestations in life, but always seek to know our origin and the final destination. Whatever exists carries some attributes of its origin; that which is real and perpetual. All the energies, lights and radiation that have emerged from singularity carry traces of that ever-present original state and reality.

Human behaviour and attributes relate to fields of energy that our mind resonates with. Anger, acceptance, rejection, generosity, love, hate and all the forces and powers that we experience are fields of energy with different characteristics and degrees of intensity and frequency of vibration. When I act generously my mind has taken on the frequency and quality of the field of generosity and good will. When I am mean then I am within the restrictive field of meanness. We naturally prefer expansion and increase and therefore prefer kindness to meanness. The brain is the physical part of our mind, which is naturally affected by subtler energy fields that bring about feelings and emotions. The human mind interacts with numerous fields of energies such as reason, rationality and other conscious and subconscious feelings and emotions.

Carbon is a key foundation for life. Every colour signals an aspect of its content and the colour that appears is the one that is absorbed, so the transmission is by omission. Black contains all the colours, red signals heat and agitation, blue brings calmness and serenity, green is soothing and reassuring. Every colour tells the story of a state.

In nature, every shape, size and colour communicates an aspect of its nature. Whatever exists has a story and the beginning of that tale is revealed through matter and energy. The challenge is to be able to read these messages and to interpret and relate to them appropriately.

Physics and metaphysics in essence are inseparable and are always complementary. Every form tells its story and that is its purpose and meaning.

Emanation And Return

Whatever begins will end. So where is the security we are seeking? We desire reliability, durability and consistency, yet no two moments are the same. What emerges will change and then vanish. The air we breathe is the precursor to that which we exhale. Every short-lived moment emerges from a previous one and gives birth to the next. Every moment is fresh and new, yet it carries with it traces of the past and points to the future. The love of the past is due to connection and familiarity. It is natural that we become nostalgic and feel grief for anything we perceive as a loss. Fear of losing is a bigger power than anticipating gain. The ultimate fear is loss of life — the ultimate cosmic treasure and grace is eternal by its timeless nature.

Change and disturbance can be frightening unless modified by experience and put in its proper context. Emanation and return leave traces within space-time, but the original energy field of oneness is ever constant and permeates the universe of diverse and changing realities. Water on earth has been recycled many times. The quantity of water on earth remains constant, it comes down, then is pulled up and filtered once again. The same filthy water, full of disease, seeps underground, is filtered by earth and then is pulled up as pure water, cycle after cycle.

Reality permeates the universe and is ever-constant, yet everything is subject to time and change. Reality appears as countless short-lived realities emanating, interacting and returning back to source. We experience all within space-time. We are within space-time, yearning for what is beyond.

We have all emerged from a mother's womb to the wider earthly womb. The first womb helped us to develop our physical and biological reality and the illusion of identity and separation. The second womb is there for us to experience countless dualities and changes, and then be propelled out of them by the desire to be at one with that which is perpetually One.

The universal challenge of life is to connect with the outer world through the lens of unity and higher consciousness from where everything had emerged. In this way we awaken to the full balance between our humanity and cosmic divinity.

THE NORM

The human drive for stability and security makes us desire durable connections with others; family, friends, people of the same lifestyle, language, religion, and other factors that bond individuals. That is the soil where the idea of normality grows. Cultural habits bring about a certain measure of expectation, stability and conduct. We have a natural tendency to define, measure and categorise what we experience. To share habits and culture and other human tendencies such as ambition, desire for good life, kindness and other emotions are considered to be normal human behaviour. Throughout human history great leaders and visionary people were considered special, even abnormal or accused of mental instability. Pricking the balloon of normality even with jokes or shocking swear words can jolt the mind and change the atmosphere of stiffness and the illusion of respectability.

Everyone tries to maintain the appearance of normality, whereas all around us there is a high level of occasional or persistent abnormality. Most minds are coloured by prejudice and ignorance and are confused due to lack of a reliable map of life's pattern. The irony is that we generally consider our wakeful state as normal whilst we cannot survive without sleep. Sleep deprivation can cause more damage to our well-being than lack of food and drink. Much healing and repair work of our mental and nervous make-up takes place during sleep.

What is accepted as normal has a strong cultural and collective value which changes at all times, often imperceptibly. Deviation from the normal is natural as part of our evolution and varies according to time and place and the factors relating to survival and improved quality of life.

Variety is the reason for adaption and the occurrence of today's human being through its evolution from basic life sentiency and animalism. In our earthly life, we strive towards perfection, however defined, and can never attain it for any durable time. Perfection itself is not limited to space or time. It emanates from the perfect essence and origin which permeates through modified versions within all of existence. Grace is cosmic and our short journey on earth propels us to recalibrate with such grace anytime and anywhere. Supremely normal — beyond all norms.

LIFE'S CHALLENGES

The one certainty in our life is the uncertainty of the future. The extent of control we have is very limited within space-time. Whatever we do now may be regretted after a while, especially with respect to emotions and feelings. It is very difficult to determine the outcome of a situation even if every effort is made toward desirable ends. Whatever is within space-time is changeable and therefore not durable or reliable. Yet we identify ourselves with the physical and biological states and agree collectively as to what is real.

Collective consciousness has a big influence over our thoughts and actions. We are confined within space-time groping for a constancy that is perpetual. This situation is fundamentally absurd. We seek reality and that which is considered true in a zone of existence whose nature is ever changing — how absurd. No two moments are ever the same and yet we expect perfect repetition and dependence — how absurd. We get bored with routine and get excited with new toys or ideas, yet we consider security and certainty as essential — how absurd. We all conspire to respect the king, the hero, or a great leader, yet anyone can be a victim of foolish behaviour or suffering from dementia. Those who do not conform are subjected to scorn and rejection. The line between insanity and genius is thin; many a time a person who was rejected as odd will be regarded as a genius later on. We feel comfortable and are at ease with others who conform to the familiar of the norm and what may be commonly considered agreeable and fits in with expectations.

The human mind draws its energy from higher consciousness but it can deviate into all kinds of absurdities. Much human destruction and bloodshed has been due to mental ideas, beliefs, fears, greed, anxieties and other animalistic tendencies. Looking at human history we can laugh and cry at the same time. Only a few see the comedy within the tragedy. Most humans are scared to discover that whatever they considered important or real is in actual fact inconsequential. The worries of a few years ago are no longer here. Even today's concerns and drives are postponed for a while when you are asleep deeply and completely nullified when you die. All endeavours become absurd compared to awakening to the all-prevailing divine Reality.

Shaykh Fadhlalla Haeri

Evolvement

With the rise of

consciousness we

experience countless

dualities and pluralities

that connect the physical,

chemical, emotional

and higher levels of

awareness.

Dualities From Unity

The metaphor of the fall of Adam from paradise can be read as the rise of consciousness of duality. First consciousness was that of absolute unity without the constraints of space or time.

All human experiences are within duality — hard and soft, comings and goings, births and deaths, good and bad. The human project is balanced between the seen and the unseen, and the outer and the inner states. All of life relates to conditioned consciousness, which draws its energy from supreme consciousness, which is beyond birth and death, being awake and asleep, the past and future. Our world has countless material entities and energies that connect, disconnect and interact. We experience life as a bushy tree of dualities emerging from the seed of singularity. The desire for connectedness and continuity are due to the primary state of our origin — Oneness.

The two lovers hug, hope and pretend to be one. We are from the One and our earthly experience is preparing us to return to the perpetual state of oneness. Death ends the experience of duality and conditioned consciousness. This world is a nursery to practise higher consciousness and oneness. We are like photons, both a particle and a wave function. Our identity as a particle is due to changing conditioned consciousness and its evolution. We are always challenged with the inherent instability of our experiences, whilst seeking the security of what is permanent. Sometimes dualities complement each other, at other times cancel or destroy each other. At all times we seek peace, harmony, and the joy of unity.

Balance brings about stability, reliability, consistency and the illusion of continuity. Yet we always seek that which is unusual and extreme — we resent being confined or trapped. Our love for extreme sports, the desire to break new records, or go beyond boundaries, are all echoes of the truth that the light in our own soul is boundless. It is perpetual, eternal, constant and beyond any evaluation of the mind or reason.

Human experiences are held between the terrestrial and the celestial, the physical and the metaphysical. Our attempt is to be balanced between dualities, whilst being energised by cosmic unity.

Evolution And Revolution

Consciousness descends from the celestial realm, energising the terrestrial. This heavenly descent arches back to an origin where beginnings and end meet in timelessness and singularity of essence. In truth, there is only that origin. Everything else emanates from it as a natural consequence of what appears as separation and distance. Within space-time everything evolves from nothingness back to source. Evolution is a natural outcome of the emergence of duality. From singularity, multiplicity and all dualities move back to singularity. Nothing is constant except the original essence and sacred oneness.

Every now and then we also experience a revolutionary burst of energy. A young child wants the sweet now, not tomorrow. The poor parent tries to bring reason to a level of consciousness that is dominated by the powerful presence of the soul. The child's ego is not developed yet. The child's mind is in a revolutionary mode and wants instant gratification — the soul is in a perfect state and has not been veiled by the lower self. The adult mind is developed to living in space-time, it therefore accepts, delays and postponements. The child's soul is not shielded yet by mind and ego. The soul is ever revolutionary. It lives in the instant, perpetually, here and nowhere, within time and beyond time.

Human nature encompasses revolutionary modes on occasions, whilst coasting along an evolutionary course. We ride on the arrow of time with all its interconnectedness to other entities in space-time, with pleasant or unpleasant shocks and surprises. We are given the opportunity to get out of the habitual lethargy that governs most of our life. Nature is so generous that no one is spared regular opportunities to wake up to the light of the soul. Our habits give the illusion of desirable continuity. Most spiritual paths prescribe the breaking of habits and stepping away from mental and emotional traps.

The soul is spontaneous, lives in a perpetual, boundless mode and is at one with divine unity. It is the lower self, which is the shadow of the soul, that desires to be like the soul — in charge. Life's direction is to transcend from self to soul, from the temporary to the perpetual — beyond any evolution or revolution.

Quality And Quantity

It is the nature of the mind to discern and describe quality and quantity of experiences and events. We cannot survive without a minimum quantity of water, yet we can choke and die in a flood; same water, different quantity and quality. A high tide can destroy or damage life whilst a glass of water quenches thirst pleasurably. The human brain developed much faster due to cooked food, but the same fire when out of control can destroy all.

Quality and quantity define what is acceptable or not in human life. It is natural for us to strive towards greater quantity of what we consider as good quality. But where will it end? How much is enough? Reason and wisdom attempts to curb greed and the love of extreme, but the heart remains discontent. How much love is enough? How much wealth is enough? How much power is enough? How long a life is enough?

Anything that is measurable is a precursor of what is immeasurable. The finite is one possibility of the infinite. Time is one aspect of timelessness or infinite time. Every quality or quantity has an origin and a destiny, with a range from the physical to the metaphysical. All human experiences are samples and metaphors of full boundless consciousness. Within the limited box of space-time, the lower self drives you on to break through it and touch upon higher consciousness, where quantity and quality vanish. It is in our world of duality and discrimination that we have these numerous categories within attraction and repulsion, which include quality and quantity. All these experiences and fields of energy will disappear with deep stillness and silence of head and heart. At that point our human conditioned consciousness connects with its origin and source.

Life begins as pure consciousness with no content but as we evolve in experiencing dualities and relating them we experience the fields of quality and quantity as part of the balancing act within space-time. A state of pure consciousness is where all discernible experiences emerge from and return to. Pure consciousness is devoid of any values and judgments and can only be accessed by transcending all sensory consciousness and human limitation.

SIGNS AND SYMBOLS

Dualities relate to the mind and the senses and create the temporary experience of separate identities along with fear of disconnectedness or discontinuity. The soul beams a light that dispels the darkness and confusion of duality and otherness. What is good or bad, or soft or hard are mere signals confirming the existence of the original Light that enables them to appear. A fully awakened being witnesses the light of Truth and eternal Oneness. The presence of an enlightened being can inevitably cause apprehension and even confusion for anyone unfamiliar with these ideas and concepts. Most people are fully immersed in conditioned and temporary states of consciousness and experience.

The normal human conditioning is the wall that blocks the view of higher or durable consciousness and what is durable and real. Sometimes the obsessive love and total absorption in the One will appear as harsh, possibly even cruel, to those beings preoccupied with the primary concerns of survival and fulfilling earthly needs. Those who live at the lower level of consciousness are in perpetual struggle and have become habituated to the lower self and ego. As for the serious spiritual seeker, s/he has one main concern, and that is to be at all times at one with the One.

The experience of sacred oneness enables your awareness and acceptance of duality and otherness in the earthly sense. It is due to these shadows, that the ever-present divine light can be discerned and experienced. Wherever there is light there will be darkness, so do not deny the darkness but seek the spark of light that illumines it. When you are illumined by your realization of the perfect presence of oneness the earthly experiences will not be dominated by fears or sorrow.

To convey this truth, symbols, metaphors and a language that uses signs and examples are used and often considered to be hard to understand. Spiritual consciousness transcends the mind's limitations. Religious scriptures are often regarded as obscure or incoherent, especially by those who do not believe in them. The ultimate natural state of the evolved human being is to dwell within this universal abode that contains all and has emerged from a Light that transcends everything and yet permeates all. Truth is the light of lights, and is discerned as sparks and beams that are diluted versions of the origin. God's light pervades all. Everything emanates from It and returns to It.

WHAT RISES WILL FALL

If the sky is the limit, will you be falling from it?

Whatever appears will also disappear. Whatever exists will return to nonexistence. Whatever is born will also die. Whatever is right contains falsehood within it. Whatever gives you pleasure can give you pain. There is no success without it carrying the seed of failure at a personal or collective level. The cycle of emanation and return is ever perpetual. It is only the speed and way of manifestation that varies. The life of a corporation is prolonged due to limited liability enabling the top executive to make big mistakes without being held personally responsible.

Changes in fashion and fading memories give us the pleasant illusion of newness and freshness. Every generation simply rides on the ferris wheel of change and its distractions. Changing times and ideas are the great deceptions that conceal the ever-present permanent. It is most refreshing to meet a cheerful yogi living a colourful life, whilst wearing the same colour saffron robe summer and winter. If the inner state is vibrant and alive you care less for the outer. The more concern you have for the outer state the more likely it is that your spiritual consciousness is at a low ebb.

Sensory experiences are bracketed between arrival and departure, stimulation and response. Stability lies in the zone of consciousness that is beyond space-time. Once our day-to-day life is stable, we look for new interests and excitements. In today's world, outer success, wealth, holidays, special occasion and parties are commonly regarded as highlights in life. Equally, we have hope and expectations of leaders and heroes whom we can identify with and look up to. But in most cases, the more we expect of a hero the more we will be disappointed. Our heroes often end up as zeros. After all, as humans we are both nothing and everything. Our bodies return to the earth and disintegrate, our minds also vanish and the soul drifts back to its origin — the source of all. So where is the hero?

If any good idea or guidance has been helpful to you in a durable sense, then it may lead you to the cosmic perpetual Truth that is beyond any description of confinement. The sacred Light is not subject to any human evaluation. It is the cause of what is up as well what is down! Truth neither rises nor falls — It always is.

Relative Judgment

The nature of the mind is to discriminate, accept or reject. The reason that bad news prevails over good news is due to our fundamental concern with survival, so we pay attention and fear losses and threats that may come from bad news. We are passionate and obsessed with life and we reject death. Mind and thoughts help with physical survival and also the drive towards arrival. Whatever the senses bring to us we try to benefit from as part of our drive for a better outcome and destiny. At the age of four you were begging for a tricycle, but when it is given to you at the age of forty you question the sanity of the uncle who presents it to you. What is a correct judgment? Our earthly existence is a shadow play of original patterns and as such they are temporary and not real — with a touch of truth only. We are constantly trying to discriminate as to what is truth and what is a lie, what is honest and what is not.

Existence emanates from and returns to the perfect point of singularity, ever at peace and stillness. Appropriate judgment is that which does not disturb the natural flow of existence but enhances the evolution of consciousness. It is human interference that may bring about irreversible changes on earth and undesirable outcomes. Our spiritual inadequacy is the cause of ecological disaster. An idea that seemed good to a people at the time may cause much regret later on as the outcome is not reversible. We desire correct judgment to reduce regrets, sorrow and suffering.

There are local judgments with minor implications and others that can have major repercussions. The most correct judgment is made when head and heart are in unison and reference is made to higher consciousness. Then you are simply reading the situation in its fullness rather than interfering clumsily. If your heart agrees with your mind, and you reflect upon the issue from the highest level of awareness, then you avoid regrets and enjoy the perfect flow of life.

We naturally prefer judging others than being judged. Often people will defend themselves by saying "you really don't understand me." They are quite right. They are also wrong because they too do not know themselves. How can you know your soul which itself is the source of all knowledge? Only your soul knows itself. Or as they say, only God knows God.

CONFUSION AND FUSION

Consciousness begins to build up early on, from a place of no content to what we hope ends up as intelligent and sensible. To begin with, the baby starts choosing, accepting and rejecting. With maturity we may end up confused by choice. This is when we become wasteful and move from functional use to frivolous choices which may be attractive for a moment, then discarded soon after. Confusion and uncertainty are among the foundations of the thinking process. We are as much confused by ignorance as by knowledge. A little knowledge is dangerous. This applies even more aptly with spiritual knowledge. People on the lower end of the spiritual ladder can cause more damage than those who have no spiritual pretence. Superstition, fear of the unknown and the desire to be with soothsayers or readers of the future can cause more harm than goodness.

Nowadays we are saved from much quackery and even dangerous use of what would have been considered as a remedy not long ago. The prevalence of the allopathic medicalisation and its vast industry is based on physical, chemical and biological sciences and as such it does work at those levels. The side effects and the danger of dependency is of course the big price that we all pay. Due to our love of power we all have the tendency of being helpful by recommending remedies to heal others from pain or illness. You have to be careful when you complain about an illness to someone else for it is likely that the hidden healer emerges to prescribe to you what he or she considers necessary for you. Playing as a doctor or teacher is a common human tendency.

We live in the confinement of space-time and the duality of causalities. No matter what we do that which involves our body, mind and emotions may be right or wrong depending on the context. Our earthly living is like travelling along a foggy terminal except for situations where cause and effect can be demonstrated clearly. Our journey on earth is from complex confusions towards another zone which is beyond duality and that is where perfection of fusion lies. The grace of this journey encompasses every living entity and the critical point that is discerned by all is the moment of death. Beyond that lies unmasked Reality or Truth.

Towards Higher Consciousness

Human beings always desire a new experience. We are on the ladder of higher consciousness whose end is cosmic consciousness or pure consciousness.

It is wonderful that we have great love and reverence for nature. We love, respect and try to be at one with nature. Our most intricate physical and biological reality has evolved in nature over millions of years. It is natural for us to love Mother Nature. The only difference between us and other species is higher awareness and consciousness of consciousness. We are part of nature but equally need to participate as a gardener to do a certain amount of housekeeping and improving. We need to learn how to knot the umbilical cord of a newly born baby. We learn how to use tools and have during the past few centuries become almost totally dependent on technology.

With the rise of the mind and intellect we are often curious as to the limits of the universe, as well as what is within the atomic world. A fully awakened being would have experienced the vastness and boundlessness of the universe and that which is immeasurable in minuteness is connected and on the path to discover oneness, which may take a multitude of paths and directions. A child's mind evolves due to desires and needs. Many religious people want to be God's agent or representative. The love of knowledge and power drives everyone towards endless illusions as to what is important for them to have a fulfilled life. Everyone desires something or another at all times. That includes the yogi in the cave who was asked by a passing being, *"I was told you don't need anything. What can I do for you?"* The answer was *"Yes, move away from the entrance. So, I too have a desire."*

To be fully awakened you need to combine all your childhood desires into one — to desire not to have any desire which is not completely possible so long as you are still connected to your body and the mind. We tend to accept the natural drive towards higher consciousness but what does it really mean and what is the end of it?

We are all climbing up ladders towards the subtler and more powerful realms of energies, yet we are uncertain as to what that means. The awakened sage declares that pure consciousness is beyond any measure of perfection, beauty or majesty. It is simply boundless joy, the ultimate gift.

Shaykh Fadhlalla Haeri

FURTHER ON

Besides the physical

evolution in creation there

is the rise in consciousness

towards the original

cosmic state. The more we

go beyond ourselves the

clearer our understanding

of Truth will be.

LIGHTS OF LIFE

The smallest entity in existence reflects the cosmic vastness. Both originate from nothingness. The two extremes emerge from the mysterious singularity!

The mystery and power of life gives rise to reflection and self-awareness. Life knows life exclusively and is self-protective. Everything that exists has a life of its own, and as such, there are countless levels, states and zones of life, some with sentiency and reflective awareness, others without what we understand as consciousness.

Minerals have their own distinct life, character, language and frequency that is transmitted as vibration. The entire universe is in a transition and evolution from singularity and timelessness as an expansion of that cosmic mystery. When the chemical and physical condition on earth reached a point of responding and interacting with the lights of consciousness, self-awareness and sentiency, then life emerged. It began as a simple semi-permeable cell a few hundred million years ago, close to the oceans. That cell related to its environment by electromagnetic chemical flow. This is the foundation of duality. Many millions of years later oxygen came about with abundance and filled the atmosphere, eventually resulting in the most complex of all life forms. Human life as a result assumed the most valuable and precious quality of Reality. Our life is delicate, whereas life itself is most powerful and permanent. It is this longevity and security that we seek and desire at all times. The human soul has that quality. As humans, however, we are perpetually preoccupied with life as it is the most precious gift given to us. Most of our efforts are to preserve life, prolong it or to improve the quality of our experiences of it.

The primary force of all life is to expand and perpetuate life itself. Complexity of life relates to the extent of consciousness that an entity carries with it. Preservation and maintenance of life is the primary obsession from which all other desires are born; the new-born baby responds to its autonomic system to feed so as to maintain life. Much of our efforts are to preserve and prolong life, whereas in truth life preserves itself. If you are willing to give up your life cheerfully then you are at the door of joy and bliss of perpetual life — as known to the soul.

Cosmic Dust

The key substances in our life — earth, water, air and fire — connect, support and balance each other. They are fundamental to the occurrence of astonishing diversities of matter, energy and consciousness. Matter emanates from energy with certain qualities and is part of the cosmic energy pool.

Fire is a living and changing bundle of matter that combusts to yield energy, light, colour and other entities. It is delicate, yet most powerful. When the fire is young, a gentle breeze will extinguish it, when it is mature and full, it will dominate and devour all that is in its path. Without fire there can be no heat, no light and no life. Without electrons or photons there would be no sentiency or life; electrons are the bloodline of our nervous system.

Air or gas is the most abundant substance in volume and is a natural space filler. It is the lightest, yet can be the most powerful, moving rocks and oceans, and causing hurricanes. Air and oxygen sustain human life, yet oxidation erodes it. Our dependence on these gases symbolise our dependency on subtler invisible ingredients within the universe. Hydrogen is the simplest and smallest atom and when fused with oxygen water is produced.

Water is commonly considered as the fundamental substance of life. It is a most unique material for it expands in volume when frozen rather than contracts like other materials. Water when frozen can crack granite and as in the case of floods or tsunamis can sweep away homes and towns in its wake. As vapour or moisture it mingles gently with the other elements. Water carries mysterious energies and traces which we may consider as memory. Our own human cells also carry the traces of our own life.

Earth and other physical matter are packages of energy frozen in a form as atoms and molecules for a while. When released, the physical qualities change and are transformed or destroyed. When the energy force within the molecule atom is released the radiation emitted can be immense. Nuclear energy releases the innermost power of matter. The Hiroshima destruction was caused by just two kilos. The human structure and form depends on numerous elements of the earth, which have their origin as stardust. We are stardust living by the cosmic Light that is both the origin and destination of all.

THE CENTRE

The universe is composed of energy and matter, and the interplay between all that exists with beginnings and ends. But where is the centre of it all? Is there any part that is ever constant? The relative stability of our earth is based on the balance between the gravitational pull towards its centre and the upward and outward centrifugal force.

The human quest to get to the heart of the matter is a natural human drive to explore and know. We discover the centre of gravity or the centre of the storm, but continue the Holy Grail to discover the centre of all. All these centres are in fact metaphors of the cosmic Centre that permeates every situation in existence. It is a Centre that is everywhere and at all times. That is the origin of the religious belief that God is everywhere at all times. Whatever exists has a physical or metaphoric centre.

We want to be at the centre and be inclusive, and resent being excluded. We want to know the centre of power and the central issue is the essential part of a debate. We want to be connected to the centre of all connections and events so as to experience contentment, security and lasting tranquillity. We are curious as to our personal centre! Is it the heart? Where is that heart? What and where is the centre of the earth? What and where is the centre of our galaxy? Will anyone experience being at one with the centre and then stop all other enquiries?

Every galaxy revolves around its black hole, where everything returns and vanishes. The human project will be fulfilled when the elusive self vanishes in its own black hole, where there is no space or time or the illusion of separation. Is there anything more desirable than a truly fulfilled love affair?

Love of life is in the centre of our existence. I am obsessed with life and that emanates from my soul within my heart. I am obsessed with my life, which is a stage that leads to the source of the universe that mysteriously permeates, governs and unifies the universe. The real Centre is everywhere and nowhere at the same time and in no time! In truth, the Centre permeates everything, and we are groping with traces of it.

ATTRACTION AND REPULSION

Our senses are intricate instruments that feel and connect what is visible and tangible to feelings and emotions. They connect the inner personal state with the world outside and enable the evolving living entity to resonate with universal Reality. The diverse sensory experiences meet and unify within an inner combining sense. Intelligence is the expression of clarity and health of these senses and their communication with each other and with a higher consciousness within a given context.

Through both our outer and inner senses, we share the experience of duality. The Truth is beyond all that, as well as within it. Every thought or movement is either attractive or undesirable. Human life is in continuous balance between acceptance and rejection. Our course of life passes through diverse narrow lanes and paths towards our destiny of awakening to origin.

The constant judgment and evaluation of every event or experience is due to our desire and need to be in balance in the moment whilst connecting past with future. A neutral attitude is in the middle of likes and dislikes. The extent of success or failure of our pursuits are as good as the quality of stillness and silence from which these impulses emerge. Deep sleep helps to recalibrate our overall state and to increase clarity of intention and reference to higher consciousness.

For most people being alone is undesirable except for those who enjoy silence, reflection and transcendence. To be alone can be a spiritual energiser. In truth you are never alone. Your soul is ever connected to the whole cosmos. Duration of quietude and stillness is important for healing, well-being and homeostasis. Equally important is regular frequency and duration of experiencing movement, activity and change.

We love music and the flow of hearing, which is even more appreciated during the intervals of silence and reflection. It is a big gift to be quiet before talking, in between and after. This is where the potency of communication lies. We seek peace and tranquillity because that is the original state from which the whole universe emerged.

SPEED AND STILLNESS

Much of our technology is derived from nature's own technology. Human inventiveness and love for ease and comfort has produced numerous inventions and possibilities that have increased our efficient connectedness, awareness and knowledge. The speed at which we have dominated the earth and multiplied human population became possible through the improvement of hygiene, diet and the quality of water and air. Material comfort and ease are sought-after globally alongside other desires and aspirations, reducing human contentment in all situations.

We are always looking for the new. We love change and desire new experiences and possessions such as houses, clothes, other needs and the paraphernalia of day-to-day life. Our materialistic way of life is much to do with our obsession with power, possession and fear of missing out on what is considered desirable. Our love for change is due to fear of being stuck in a static situation. This desire to get out of the box of limitations of space-time propels us to desire speed and instant gratification. To get out of conditioned consciousness we need to get beyond the speed of light. This is very speedy, 300,000 kilometres per second. Surely to stop completely with no thought or movement is an easier way to experience timelessness. Our age now is that of speed, but a few people appreciate the wisdom of stillness, silence and deep meditation. With mindfulness and mindlessness you are at the zone of full consciousness, sacred consciousness or God consciousness. In our so-called normal world everybody wants instant contentment, instant achievement and instant healing, yet we carry on acquiring new desires and new complicated illnesses. Then, we complain and blame others for our suffering. The wise seeker knows that less is more and that desire for instant gratification has its roots in the truth that the soul is perfect without needs, and that the pain we feel due to its shadow, the self, is only there to help us out of this cul-de-sac. Everything has emanated from absolute peace and returns to it. The downside of speed is that you get exhausted and never reach the garden of your own soul. The innate desire to get to the end of the story is an echo of the design that takes us back to the origin from where all begins. Now is forever and is not subject to stillness or speed. Truth is ever there — everywhere!

LOCALITY AND UNIVERSALITY

All human experiences begin as local but move towards wider and deeper vistas. From the unseen, energies emerge as subatomic particles, molecules and more complex physical entities. Energy and matter are interchangeable and inseparable. The small corner shop with some interesting products soon may end up as a national chain or a globally desired franchise. Our consciousness begins in the most local and specific fashion, and grows furiously, curious to discover and investigate boundlessness. The sky is not the limit. We want to know what is the other side of the universe. The inner soul knows all of this and the mind is its investigating agent. We are driven towards wider and deeper consciousness. We are driven to get out of locality towards universality. We love expansion and increase, sometimes to the point of breakdown.

The foetus in the womb is very local, but the new-born baby is less local and soon is driven to explore and understand its immediate environment. What is it looking for?

Every one of us begins as local and limited whilst questioning what is universal and boundless. We constantly strive and struggle. Why? How? And by what authority?

To get close to boundless consciousness we need to transcend all mental and sensory states. It is in human nature to desire altered states of consciousness, even though it is temporary and can come with undesirable side-effects.

When universality is experienced and reliably accessed, then locality is appreciated and accepted as an earthly pastime. The perfume of the rose began its journey in mud, water and compost. When you live as a soul or spirit you do not denounce the lower self or ego. The self and its changing identity is local, whereas the soul and spirit is cosmic. The self loves to collect and control whilst the soul is perpetually content with its own light resonating with universal governance, where the beginning and end become inseparable and good and bad vanish by equalising each other out. All that remains are unknown perfections and pure consciousness.

❧

Natural Uncertainties

Why do we consider life's duration as short? Even if you double the average age that question will still be asked. If life on earth began one year ago then Homo sapiens would have come about a few seconds ago. There are also ever-increasing global uncertainties and problems with human beings adding fear and sorrow to it. Where do all difficulties arise from and how do they end? Surely it is to do with our human expectations and desires to bring about a better world. New situations arise as a result of our intentions and actions but often with unintended consequences.

Questions such as contentment, happiness, joy, and other related feelings and emotions all relate to a flow in life that is harmonious and constantly calibrated to perpetual cosmic life. We are often concerned with world peace, the environment and other issues relating to our temporary earthly home. Zillions of cosmic rays and other forces remind us how vulnerable our own life is. The value we give to time and the urgency to wake up to higher consciousness now is more powerful than all other ideas and endeavours. Global peace will prevail when we are fully at peace with ourselves and at one with our souls. By doing so, we are no longer an additional burden to Mother Earth and we will have completed the real purpose for which we were given the illusion of independent intention and action. To be fully present in the moment is the most important and urgent task. This needs to be attained.

Another serious question is death and the hereafter. We like to be hopeful and expect tomorrow to be better than today and that life after death will be better than our daily struggles and uncertainties. Many people benefit from faith and/or belief in religious promises. The hereafter is the zone where space-time ceases functioning and none of us will have any will or power to act. That zone of timelessness is also accessible now and can be experienced if we switch off our consciousness of space-time.

To transcend our senses needs practice but the benefits are immense for those committed to the challenges of managing that experience. Our normal earthly experiences prepare us to rise in consciousness by regular higher reference and perspective. All challenges, desires and hopes vanish when we can transcend our body and mind at will. This is the real universal challenge for all.

DENIAL AND ACCEPTANCE

In our world of dualities there is a beautiful intricate balance between all opposites. Love and hate of something or another is perpetual. One scale goes up, the other goes down and the meeting point is a spot that doesn't move. That is where two opposites become one.

The most frequently uttered word by a child is "no". It exasperates the parents. The tired mother wants some harmony and acceptance, while the child's mantra is "no". In a way, subconsciously the child is rejecting duality and separation. The ego and the mind have not yet developed to filter out the celestial power of unity emanating from its own soul. If the child wants something it wants it now because the concept of space-time has not yet been fully internalised.

The soul is perpetually present, whereas the mind begins to understand the limitations of conditioned consciousness and space-time. The rejection of a baby's defiance is natural, and with experience, its acceptance and acquiescence is also natural, as it desires harmony and the mother's acceptance. We are propelled along the forces of connection and continuity through our evolving consciousness and its source — supreme consciousness.

Most of the time we are either accepting or rejecting, and our ultimate reference point and calibration is the soul, with its unconditional love and life force. Each one of us experiences limitations and dualities with an occasional touch of the higher voltage of supra consciousness and oneness. We are rejecters of the trap of limitations and desire the boundless. Our soul calls us to itself, whereas the shadow self distracts us.

Each one of us is inclusive and exclusive in its existence and its heavenly perfection and earthly manifestation. Within our earthly experience no two people are the same at any time, and this is where the exclusion zone comes in. In what matters most, we are all included. We may say that God loves all His creation equally. Yet, you and I don't love other people equally or constantly. Everything that exists will change. That is where limits and boundaries play their part. We want to be included in what is desirable, and fear, reject or exclude death and the unknown. We accept what we know and love, deny what we don't. We say "yes" to the self as a child and with wisdom say "no" to the self especially when the light of the soul is being discovered.

HEAD, HEART, MIND AND SOUL

It is often said that the heart knows all, but how do you know the heart? How can you distinguish between transient feelings or emotions and that which is inspired or reliably intuitive? Clear mind and intelligence are important to relate efficiently with the sensory world. The mind is the link between the rest and me, and that includes my soul and the world we live in. To deal with outer life you need a clear mind, but to connect with life itself you need a pure heart.

The human heart is a most delicate faculty that needs constant purification and polishing. It rusts easily and once it is clogged the light of the soul will not shine efficiently through to body and mind. The soul draws its life from the cosmic source, then beams it to the body and mind via the channels of the heart. The pure heart beams the light of the soul and its cosmic Reality on the physics and chemistry of the human entity, connecting the source of personal life and consciousness to the discernible person as body, mind, and identity. It is a junction between the Infinite and the finite; absolute Truth and ever-varying relative and changing situations.

Important discoveries are always made as part of creative insights and openings from the heart. The mind functions within the field of dualities and it needs its fair share of rest in order to be recharged by the soul. Emotional instability and psychological disturbances can be improved by recharge through higher consciousness and a wholesome heart, which is the source of healing and well-being. Healthy life is that which is in balance between head and heart and the illumined life that radiates from the soul.

Most human quests can be traced to the one question, who am I? We cannot deny the physical, chemical and biological realities of who we are, but anything that changes is not reliable, and we remain insecure. You can access who you really are through the heart and that is the home of your soul or spirit, a reflection of divine Reality, perpetual, constant and ever present. That is who you really are. The awakened being considers the rationality and reason of the mind, then reflects upon the soul for approval. The so-called you is only a shadow or an image of your soul which is the source of durable spiritual wisdom — where fear, sorrow and guilt are eliminated.

Shaykh Fadhlalla Haeri

Humans

Much of our conscious

life relates to physical,

emotional and spiritual

well-beingness.

At all times we are obsessed

with life and its multi-faceted

connectedness.

Life itself is beyond any

limitation and is ever continuous.

The awakened being realises the

inseparability of personal life

from its cosmic origin.

SPECTRUM OF CONSCIOUSNESS

The first two decades of human life are primarily dominated by physical, biological and mental growth and development. Adulthood brings with it yearning for greater knowledge and achievement. Within a few months of birth, consciousness such as emotions and feelings develop. Conditioned consciousness grows and becomes more complex over the years. Personality and identity backed up by memories and values become more definable. The divine spirit within is boundless and beyond rigidity or flexibility. Physical growth and maturity is a natural phenomenon that all human beings experience, but spiritual awakening and the experience of full consciousness is rarely attained during this life but everyone will wake up to soul consciousness after death.

Even when we refer to someone being fully conscious, we are still talking about confinement to the limitation of space-time. Yearning for higher consciousness implies the hope and desire to be awakened to a level of consciousness beyond human limitations. It is to be conscious of consciousness, conscious of consciousness of consciousness, *ad infinitum.* Complete consciousness is consciousness with no content. That is what some people equate to God consciousness or supreme consciousness. When that state is experienced then all other conditions that are considered important will begin to fade away. In truth the purpose of human life is to awaken to complete consciousness before death. Without that realisation there will be a serious shock and confusion with death.

Conditioned and complete consciousness make up the full spectrum of realities. All human experiences relate to these two zones of consciousness. As humans, we need rationality and reason, and as souls we experience an energy which is beyond what can be described. One zone is evolving, changing, conditioned and limited, while the other is boundless, timeless and devoid of discernible content; it is pure, absolute and sacred.

We carry the full spectrum of consciousness containing humanity and divinity within our own soul and as such there is total inner spiritual reliance and our experiences in the outer world are to be referred back to the inner soul. God's light is within us but we are mostly concerned with the latest mental or physical stimulation.

RELATIONSHIPS

Everything in existence comes in twos and multiples that complement, balance or cancel each other. Nothing is in isolation and the entire universe is a complex bundle of obvious and hidden interdependence. All levels of relationships and connections flow in harmony that relate to human reason, intellect and beyond.

Our day to day relationships with others is a continuous challenge unless we refer to higher consciousness, understanding, acceptance, respect and presence of mind and heart. Most people do not recognise a real friend nor a serious enemy. For a child, a friend is an agreeable playing companion and an enemy is whoever dominates or spoils the game. For a mature person, a friend reflects what is true or real, even if it is not pleasant. Then there is the possible switch between enmity and friendship. One day a friend may become an enemy and vice versa. It depends on context and circumstances. Spiritual progress becomes evident when the seeker is with least prejudice and regards other humans as potential friends. That state is the outcome of recognising the sameness of all souls and their sanctity. In normal human relationships we are within conditioned consciousness. To be kind to the animal-self of your friend is to the detriment of his soul and to warn against the ego self is to the advantage of higher consciousness. The process of evolving towards higher consciousness is enhanced by seeing the light of oneness within otherness. To have any company or relationship is better than having none. To challenge judgment and values can help consciousness to rise higher. Everything leads back to the original sacred oneness. That source is the divine light within your own heart and if human relationship is in constant harmony with that reality then no other relationship will be abhorrent. When a relationship is in unison then the quality of conditioned consciousness is enhanced with least fear or sorrow.

Every relationship brings with it pleasure as well as pain. With divine grace and the light of your own soul, you may be able to transcend to a state that is beyond pleasure and pain, good and bad, earthly and heavenly. You are close to cosmic consciousness and that is the purpose and meaning of human drive and real hope and aspiration. One can only be really content and happy when the relationship between body, mind and heart are in perfect harmony.

FAMILY, FRIENDS AND OTHER BONDS

Individuals survive and thrive by being connected with other beings. The inventions and tools of digital technologies have speeded up global interconnectedness. The source of what unifies and holds the human species together is the spiritual fabric of all souls, giving rise to similar tendencies, desires and evolving consciousness towards origin. We long to belong with family, friends and those with whom we share similar thoughts, aspirations, language, religion and culture. These various bonds increase our security, fulfilment and contentment.

Human connectedness is at numerous levels, including physical, material, chemical, biological, emotional and subtler consciousness. Empathy, compassion and love are obvious forces that propel us towards wider points of connectedness and unity. The natural desire to seek approval is a reflection of the unconditional love of the soul. The life energy that radiates from a soul is unconditional and exclusive to every individual. This life force is the same for all.

With empathy, human beings can imagine the state of another person and resonate with it. To connect with that which appears to be different and diverse is a natural force that drives us towards greater spiritual discoveries and original cosmic singularity. As all souls are similar, we seek sameness in others, which reflects the perfect constancy of original oneness. Everything has emerged from the One and returns to the One. The feeling of loneliness and need of companions or partners can bring about a better understanding of spiritual sameness and differences in body and mind. The soul that we seek actually resides within the heart.

Life on earth is an exercise in discerning original oneness while perceiving existence through the lens of duality. No one is spared this challenge and no intelligent person can also deny the desire to get beyond the limitations of conditioned personal consciousness, which is the cause of differentiation, bias, preferences and judgments. We are driven to connect but what we really seek is that original singularity and cosmic gatheredness before the dispersion of the universe. The nature of the soul contains that state.

DUTIES AND RESPONSIBILITIES

Caring is optimum when your heart is pure and is motivated by love. To be dutiful and responsible is natural to most human beings and its source is concern and love for one's own self. You owe it to yourself to know who you really are so that you function optimally. You need to understand the meaning and purpose of your own life, which is to be in unison with the source of cosmic life itself. From that root arises a hierarchy of duties and responsibilities ranging from one's own self, other creations, and indeed the whole of existence. The brief human experience of earthly life will be wasted without a focus as to the meaning, purpose and its direction. Honesty, reliability and loyalty all follow from accepting the premise that we need personal will to rise along the arc of consciousness towards the source — divine or cosmic consciousness. With this reference, the appropriateness and hierarchy of duties and responsibilities follow.

The numerous kinds and levels of duty include the physical, material, emotional and spiritual. We need to give the right attention and concern for a healthy body, mind and heart. Once our attunement to humanity is in a reasonable state then the original drive to discover the divinity will become prominent.

We have a duty towards investigating and discovering the shifts in consciousness that take place during our lifetime, as well as after death. We understand the importance of deep sleep and the importance of concentration and focus during wakeful times. Our ultimate duty is to realise the cosmic source of life that encompasses all that is in the universe. This is the challenge and purpose that faces every human being.

Good action implies less of yourself and more of your soul. The rest are shadows and veils. Good action draws its light from your soul through the channel of a purified heart and is not deflected or poisoned by mental dualities or otherness. It occurs with ease and just flows through you. You are not making a special conscious effort or being consumed by difficulty. It is a flow of light and energy that ends all illusions of separations. Your own contentment and its duration is a function of you being fully present in the moment, whilst in a wakeful state.

Pleasing Others

Pleasure implies easy flow and we like that. We naturally prefer harmony to discord. We constantly experience descent and ascent in consciousness. Sometimes we are mean and selfish, at other times we act with generosity and goodwill. We always hope to connect smoothly and favourably with the situation we are in. We enjoy being pleased with ourselves and others but the self changes and so do others. Yet we desire stability!

Most of us struggle, personally and for the sake of others to bring about well-being without which we are in greater disturbance and chaos. It is not enough if I am just pleasing myself because at no time is one in complete isolation from the environment and independent from other human beings. Without family and other people our species will be extinct. The well-being of others is next to the importance of personal well-being. It is not good enough to be healthy and content while surrounded by unhappy creatures who are moaning, groaning and living in physical and mental disorder. If you feel good, you like to share it. You like to acquire beautiful objects to show and share them and if you are greedy enough you will be called a philanthropist and have a museum housing your art collection named after you.

You have no option but to want the best for yourself and others. When your cup is full it spills over but for a generous person he shares his cup with others even when almost empty. An awakened person welcomes others to look at themselves in their hearts' mirrors, by shining a torch that enables others to light their candles.

The soul's light is cosmic and all we need to do is to experience how darkness naturally vanishes when light appears. No two-finger prints are the same but the function of a finger and its importance are the same. A healthy person cannot help wanting well-being and goodness for all. In truth, otherness is the outer earthly package of cosmic oneness. Existence of otherness is the nursery that enables the grooming and blossoming of one's own self. We are all the same in essence, having emerged from cosmic oneness and on our way back to it, whilst experiencing differences and changes. I am living as a soul when I see all others as potentially the same as me. That state is most pleasing for all.

GROOMING THE LOWER SELF

Human life and the evolution of consciousness implies acceptance of qualities considered to be virtuous and turning away from what slides us back into lower levels of consciousness which we term as vices. The lower self needs to express itself, then yield to the soul for transformation to take place. Most intelligent beings try to climb out of lower levels of confusion to higher zones of knowledge and insights. It is like climbing the ladder of limited and conditioned consciousness towards pure consciousness.

If religion doesn't lead to that zone of consciousness, then it becomes the flag of war we kill each other for. Religion can be a rocket that propels you to the soul and the origin of life, or becomes a dungeon of fears and sorrows. Your humanity flourishes with comfort, ease, friendship and community, but with it also comes egotistic conflict and social discord. Earth for us is like a noisy and sometimes dangerous block of apartments. We start from the lower level and climb up the religious ladder with hope and expectations of one day reaching the roof garden. If you pause near each floor you naturally witness the horror of confusions, camouflaged as normality. Those who reach the roof garden forget about the ladder because of the staggering beauty of perfection where heaven and earth meet in perfect beauty and harmony. But those who stay on the ladder want the dwellers to admire the ladder. They want to propagate their religion, culture and life's habits. To proselytise is proof that you are not overwhelmed by the perfect garden.

For spirituality to blossom, you need to turn away from your natural, physical and biological biography. Many spiritual seekers make radical changes in their human habits, which may include religion, culture, career and other conditions.

Early on, your past interests, beliefs and personal engagement enabled you to develop, but now they are distractions. When you lose yourself and your past, what remains is the ever-present cosmic light within, the thrilling music of life. It sings for you, to stop all anxieties, fears and sorrows. That music declares the divine Presence. All else was protection or the outer shell of a treasure that only those who are at one with it, know and live it. Those who just think of it or aspire for it are simply on a path towards it.

The Individual And The Collective

Duality and plurality prevail. Multiplicity increases, diversifies and becomes more complex. Life began in a single semi-permeable cell a few hundred million years ago, now there are billions of creatures with each living entity concerned with preserving and propagating its life. We are obsessed with love of life and consider it the most precious entity. Buffaloes feel safer and more secure when in a herd than when alone. There is safety in numbers, as well as other beneficial advantages. If you are part of a herd you don't have to run faster than the lion, you just have to run faster than the slow ones. A hopeless situation becomes tolerable. With concentration of people, productivity and creativity also increase. Specialisations and economies of scale are amongst the many natural desirable outcomes of groups. The natural tendency to compare oneself with others increases the personal drive towards excellence and better performance.

Cross-cultural connectedness between groups of people can enhance the quality of life through natural selection. The issue of otherness is balanced between what is good for progress and the evolution of consciousness and what is considered a hindrance.

Within a few hours of conception, the foetus vibrates and soon after the heart begins to beat. Then, there are a number of momentous changes in the womb culminating in the major event of emergence into the outer world. The lifeline of the umbilical cord is now replaced with numerous other connecting mechanisms: air, food, retention, expulsion, stimulation and response through all the senses. Then there are numerous shifts in physical growth as well as consciousness. With puberty come sexual desires and other rapid chemical, physical and psychological changes. The story of human growth and maturity mirrors that of the universe. The fundamental foundation of the universe was laid out within the earliest few seconds.

Individual and collective life follows a similar script of inception, maturity, decline and end. For thousands of years groups of humans migrated, mingled, increased in number and then split again with survival and propagation as the main objective. A few beings experienced higher or pure consciousness and influenced others as prophets, and awakened or enlightened beings.

WHOSE AUTHORITY?

From ancient times human beings hoped and expected their rulers to be superior in ability, knowledge and power with access to the unseen. The king was considered to be God's representative on earth. That idea gave rise to the notion of the divine right of kings! The rule of a strong king or emperor brought some stability and continuity based on belief, trust and acceptance. A child shuns authority unless it emanates from someone loved and trusted. An adult appreciates legitimate authority because it brings about greater efficiency or improvements to the quality of life. We also will denounce it wherever it is unjust or not conducive to a wholesome quality of life.

We admire lasting authority as it replicates continuity and ongoingness of life. Ultimate authority is Divine and can be accessed through the soul, which is a mirror of the cosmic Soul. God is the one and only Author of the universe. Legitimate authorship is a modified or diluted version of the cosmic Author. The question is how to recognise when you are truly following that ultimate Authorship? How do you know that it is the voice of Truth in you rather than your ego? What about your fear of others? What about your desire to please others? What about your desire to avoid sorrow? We love to speak with authority. The self or ego likes to speak on behalf of the authority of the soul. Your ego is less dominant when the highest level of consciousness is your authority. You are then close to the voice of Truth.

Human life and experience emerge from countless unfolding of miracles. What is unknown and unknowable supersedes all we know in quantity and quality. Who is it that moved your hand? Why do you have this thought and not another? Who is the real Author and the Master? Why do you want to act with the least regrets or sorrow for the future? We all share the illusion of independence and free will to make up our own mind. Surely the mind simply confirms the decision that has already been made by the billions of neurons within your guts and your subconscious by the autonomic system. The ultimate Author is cosmic and universal, as well as local. The light of life in your own heart — your own soul is the local representative of the cosmic Author!

Drive For Excellence

Whatever exists within space-time has a built-in imperfection as it is always subject to change. No matter what you do contains an element of imperfection with an underlying aspiration toward perfection. The nature of the mind is to respond to stimulations and to connect appropriately with the outer world. A disturbed mind lacks direction, clarity of task and knowledge. The mind is alive when challenged and focused on an outcome. Any task you undertake can be elevated so that it becomes both enjoyable and has a higher meaning when undertaken with passion, dedication and focus. If you can postpone the concern for the outcome and just immerse yourself with love and dedication, then you enter into a zone of high achievement and inspiration.

As humans, we look forward to healthy growth. There is a big difference between stillness and stagnation, and between natural growth and cancer. Stagnation leads to disintegration and a return to original basic elements, whilst growth implies hope and a journey towards evolved outcome. Without desire for outcomes there will be little earthly growth, yet there will be no awakening unless the idea of outcomes themselves is given up. We are always driven towards excellence, efficiency, speed and the least waste of time or material. In life there are those who excel in performance and output and those who try to camouflage inefficiency and blame others or circumstances. The drive for excellence requires much discipline and effort. Obsession with perfection is like a beam from the soul that is ever perfect. That perfection reveals itself with or without effort.

Our desire for excellence and to achieve makes us seek teachers, knowledge and spiritual realisation. When the goal is awakening to higher consciousness we try to evaluate our spiritual progress and grade religious or spiritual teachers along a scale of awakening or enlightenment. Everybody in truth is enlightened at heart, but you need to submerge your head, mind, body, memory and your past biography into that light within your own heart, the ever-perfect soul.

Up To Date

The human soul is timeless and everything that emanates from it carries traces of its sacred origin. Whatever we experience in time is not good enough since our real nature is timeless. That is the root of the desire for the ever-perpetual and the latest now.

Our interest in antiquities is part of our curiosity about our origin. The 3000-year-old Greek earrings are given value and respect because of our reverence for the ancient.

Every one of us is the product of the past while remaining puzzled by that past, by the present and the future. We are all reading the present and hope for a better future. We have an innate natural belief that if you are fulfilled now then the future cannot be less in quality.

I want the latest news so as to be connected with the latest events — not only local but also global. Everyone is born in a very specific time to a specific mother, then everyone seeks to be universal with more possibilities and durability. What is the point of striving to display a newly discovered precious stone that is now fashionable but will eventually return to being an ordinary pebble? Boredom is a natural drive within us towards a zone beyond change and loss. Whatever you discover and make familiar becomes the step towards a new discovery. Much of what we experience is like passing shadows. We know that in truth there is timelessness and everything else is a pathway to that reality, basking as its invisible doer.

We want to love now and hope the future will be better but what is best is a state that is ever there. As was the past, as is the present, as forever.

Love is connectedness and unity and that is the ultimate future — present now. Unconditional love transmits constancy of power that emanates from one's own soul. Our earthly life is work in progress. It is the nursery where the swing between opposites and every experience is bracketed between a beginning and an end. Our conditioned consciousness with its earthly limitations has emerged from the limitless zone of Reality, Itself. It implies lack of unison with the effluent light not subject to earthly shadows or clouds. Desiring the latest is desiring the now that is timeless and that is the state of one's own soul. All that we desire is to cut across all of the mental and emotional images of past memory and to be at one with the eternal soul.

The Human Microcosm

The human being is a most complex composition. The integrated body, mind, heart and soul carry the whole story of the universe. It connects and resonates with all physical, chemical, biological, electromagnetic forces and whatever else exists in the universe. The human being is a microcosm that replicates the universe, and contains all the different elements and processes that exist and function on the earth and beyond. This includes purifying, cleansing, leaching, changing, beginnings, endings, inclusions, exclusions, metamorphosis, food synthesis, and its deconstruction to rebuild, repair and maintain the human structure. The body relates to the mind and heart.

Human life begins with the simplest form of life and evolves into a complex awareness along several levels and dimensions. It is the outcome of numerous states of consciousness that activate the sensory faculties and a large network of neurons and electrochemical links.

Life emanates from the soul, which energises the mind, which in turn connects and activates the physical and material body with all its organs and satellites like the stars and planets in a galaxy —

all revolving around the unknown all powerful black hole, the soul itself! The heart connects the boundless celestial realms with the limited terrestrial realities. Our earthly experiences are balanced between the limitations of dualities and the endless spiritual Reality.

The soul connects with the mind through the heart. For this reason, we need to retain a clean and healthy body, a clear mind and a pure heart in order for the soul or spirit within to charge and energise the human being. When we experience health and wholesomeness in body, mind and heart, we are recharged by higher consciousness and the timeless cosmic Reality. This is where the microcosm "I" resonates with the macrocosm — Cosmos.

This is where the self loses its illusion of independence, to the soul. This is where unity celebrates oneness. This is where humanity functions through its source — divinity.

Unique Offering

The human mind is designed to seek connectedness, appropriate relationships and balance. We like to compartmentalise and pigeon-hole experiences and events.

We are always looking for what is abnormal, unused or new. The flow of nature itself follows perfect order, even though it may not appear to be so. We love pleasure and avoid pain, yet we know they are always inseparable. We condemn poison, yet it can be a crucial remedy. We try to be free of care, yet much of our energy is spent in caring for someone or another or some idea or another. We are designed to care and that is replicating the unconditional love and care of our own soul.

Much of our effort and hope is to avoid suffering and discord. That simply means we want to flow in a natural way towards our ultimate destiny where whatever could be distinguished or measured has vanished into its original state of pure cosmic consciousness.

Earthly experiences cannot be without expectations, judgments and therefore suffering. Only a few most fortunate beings straddle the full spectrum of consciousness where good and bad are acknowledged and transcended to the higher zone of cosmic consciousness that is beyond human limitations. In fact the biggest human challenge is to combine doing what you can to reduce suffering and distractions, whilst acknowledging its evolutionary benefit in the drive of consciousness towards its original and perpetual pure consciousness.

Every human being has a beginning and an end. Most people have no idea about the map of life and that birth and death are like inseparable twins. Most people try to postpone the important question of the nature of death and the experience of the hereafter. The ultimate divine grace is the realisation that life is forever and that is the most unique generous offering — your soul is timeless and to identify with anything other than that leads to suffering, confusion and depression.

Most sufferings are short lived but the most pervasive one is the question of real identity and the cosmic nature of the soul. Multiple sufferings and the sacred offering of that cosmic oneness are ever together. This is the most beautiful majestic gift — Thank you God!

LIFE

It is human nature to love life

more than anything else.

The most precious experience

is life's presence and sentiency.

The challenge for everyone is to

move beyond limited personal

life and realise the origin of

boundless life itself.

The Human Cycle

Cycles of earthly life begin with birth and end with death but can be divided into different periods.

The first of three periods is the emergence of the physical baby from the womb of the mother into the earthly womb of dualities and cycles. Whatever exists in the universe has its mirror image of what is considered opposite or complimentary, and there are different degrees of this pattern of duality. Within the earthly zone, the mind and all the intricate connections to the nervous system and conscious and subconscious begin to develop and evolve, leading to the identity of a child and the subsequent personality of a teenager and older person.

The second period is when we reflect upon our conflicting emotions, feelings and ever-changing desires. A child follows whimsical feelings but a mature person may evaluate and discard frivolous desires and irrational wishes. We learn how to balance the ego with a more measured consciousness that is reflected back to us by the mirrors of other adults around us within a particular culture or religion. We begin to put things in perspective aiming for durable goodness and contentment.

The third period is that of maturity, balance, inner reliance and higher consciousness. This state considers and understands traditional teachings from previous cultures and other people; all of which are confirmed within one's own heart by excluding mental and emotional distractions. The pure heart is the inner mirror that reflects the truth, even if that may not always be pleasant to us. Truth emanates from the divine presence, which we refer to as the soul or spirit within the heart. That is where meditation, silence, other spiritual habits and practices uplift us.

Our earthly life enables us to exercise the mind and develop higher intellect, reason and rationality, then go beyond that to spiritual wisdom, insights and knowledge that connect the seen and the unseen. If the body is healthy, the mind is clear and the heart is pure, then you live the moment with such intensity and joy that you flow along the harmony and goodness that is around you. What began as hope and aspiration is now trust and unison with your own soul. Your cycle is now complete — from confusion to fusion.

THE DRIVE TO DISCOVER

Humans love to explore, wonder and be amazed by the unexpected connectedness in the natural world. We are constantly seeking hidden causalities, relationships or connections. We are naturally driven towards higher consciousness and the pattern and flow of life and existence.

The natural drive to discover and know is empowered by our origin, which is intrinsic to all of creation. Diversities, dualities and multiplicities all emanate from and return to the energising source. At the primary zone of essence, there is no differentiation. As existence emerges everything begins to show ever-changing identities and qualities. This is the story of oneness camouflaged as otherness within space-time. The human quest to investigate, discover and know is driven by the force and presence of the original all-encompassing oneness itself.

Exploration is part of the search for oneness. All desires to discover flow towards cosmic oneness. Our attitude to push ourselves to go beyond our confinements is natural. Ordinarily boredom or impatience reflect the natural drive to experience and understand new connections and knowledge, which ultimately leads to spiritual reflections and awakening to pure Presence, beyond any boundaries or limitations.

Durable contentment in human life is sustained due to the experience of life through the lens of oneness. We begin life's experience by feeling separation, then differences and evaluations. Our personal and conditioned consciousness continues to grow and evolve with the influence of personal and other social and environmental factors. The original cosmic power of oneness that gives rise to all of our transitory earthly life drives us constantly back to it. Human short-lived life is a mere reflection of eternal life itself. We develop personal experiences and an identity only to lose all to the ever-present Reality. Cosmic Reality, Truth or God permeates the whole universe, and it is through consciousness that we end up with that discovery and realise that the beginning and end are ever present in the timelessness of the moment. The vastness of pure consciousness is that state where there is nothing known or unknown. It only Is — Ever Present.

PURPOSE AND MEANING OF LIFE

An honest person often admits to not knowing the nature, purpose and direction of his/her own life. Who am I? Where am I? Why am I here?

Most of our serious questions and challenges arise due to the illusion of separation from perpetual reality. The mind needs to reject or accept, therefore we will barely survive if we don't think that we are useful or loved. The surgeon who amputates a leg is also congratulated for saving a life. The act itself is bloody and looks brutal but the idea behind it is considered humane. An intelligent person will have experienced thousands of occasions where the purpose and meaning had changed. Where there is love, there is hate. What you consider most desirable and good may later be cause for grief and regrets. So where does all that confusion lead us? You cannot live without a purpose and you are confused by ever-changing purposes. This situation is natural within the confines of space-time, a cauldron of energy and matter interchanging and interacting in predictable and unpredictable ways. The drive behind all action is a primal force to move us from conditioned consciousness towards higher consciousness. If your concern is with higher consciousness and to transcend the limited sensory realm, then you are acting as your own midwife for a second birth and awakening to the timelessness and perpetuity of life. Spiritual evolvement implies a change in habits and all aspects relating to conditioned consciousness, both at a personal level as well as communal. Acknowledging your past, culture, race, religion and other issues is necessary before you try to transcend them towards higher consciousness.

Pure consciousness relates to the origin of life, before it had manifested as human life or animal or plant. All human drives point towards a state of consciousness that is beyond the normal. The purpose of every human life is to realise the supremacy and permanency of life itself. To realise this reality and truth you need to leave behind every thought and feeling or conditioned consciousness. It is by transcending all your senses that you enter the zone of supreme consciousness and by that you have fulfilled the work in progress that you have been subjected to in your short life on earth. Now your personal life is truly at home with your permanent life and you have fulfilled your intended destiny.

BALANCE AND BEYOND

In normal life we need healthy connectedness and balance between our physical, chemical, biological and psychological states. We are in constant change, yet we seek constancy and reliability at the same time. We are perpetually receiving and transmitting stimulation from numerous entities and countless energies that come to us from our solar system, as well as the space beyond. There are countless balancing acts that take place within us and around us, most of which we are unaware of. Much of our attention is upon the gross and sensory side of our existence. What about the unconscious that plays such a big role in our day-to-day life?

The dynamics of life are between the seen and the unseen, the terrestrial and celestial. Much of our regrets and sorrow relate to our mistakes and errors of understanding and judgment that point out the way towards higher consciousness and awakening to reality.

The outer universe is expanding and yet it has an innate stability and integrity that hints at its own soul. We also grow, expand and change, yet we refer to ourselves as "I" at all times implying certain constancy. Referring to oneself as "I" is constant and yet there is a big difference between a five-year old calling himself "I" and the fifty-year old.

Human life is in balance between interaction and change, whilst seeking the reliability and constancy of a core that is the inner soul. To be in constant reference to the light of the soul you need to be liberated from mental and emotional blockages. It is of great help to practise the art of forgiving and forgetting, going beyond guilt and sorrow, to be in touch with supreme consciousness.

Balance belongs to the earthly zone of conditioned consciousness and the boundaries of space-time. We seek ease, comfort and relief, yet the only reliable constant ease is that of being at one with one's own soul. Everything else is a challenge that is often considered an undesirable difficulty to be avoided. Pure consciousness is beyond all values or balance. It is pure, cosmic and gives rise to conditioned life and the balance between opposites. Normal day to day consciousness, thoughts and feelings require balance and calibration, whereas higher consciousness at its peak is beyond duality and balance.

ME, ME, ME FOREVER

Conventional wisdom is to allow a child to develop the ego and exercise the animal-self with responsible guidance and parental care. Grooming the ego-self with sympathetic consideration, kindness, love and generosity may enhance the ego but equally helps higher awareness of the lower self. The parents are pleased with the child who is considerate of others, helpful and respectful. Many living creatures have empathy, even altruism. The original animal-me can lead to a more evolved me but where is the end of that pursuit? A mature and wise person tries to pursue charitable causes considered by the prevailing culture to be commendable. To help and serve those who are less fortunate brings about desirable emotions and life force. The so-called "me" is a mistaken identity and the real "me" is my soul that is unconditional in love and life. To act as a soul is the essence of spiritual progress.

The origin of the ego and selfish conduct is the divine light itself — filtered, diluted and modified. The power of the light of the soul is so immense that it can only function when it is reduced in intensity and potency. It is only with the numerous atmospheric barriers that the light that reaches the earth is conducive for life. The mind and the ego are the filters that enable the soul to function and energise the body and mind. Cosmic consciousness and light need to come down from their quantum abode with reduced intensity before earthly dualities and human life can occur.

Consciousness is like a ladder stretching from the rocky earth to the other end of the universe, from basic limited consciousness and life to its cosmic source that engulfs all. Balanced consciousness leads to mature and appropriate awareness where peace and quietude are most desirable states. Why do you want peace and silence? That state is the nearest to singularity or pure consciousness before specific strands of consciousness arose. The ultimate me, therefore, is the same as the original me which is pure light of consciousness itself and its source is my own soul. The self is only a shadow of that soul which can distract me with chronic self-obsession and dark self-illusions. Awakening means being at one with the soul, ever present, ever perfect and ever-joyful. What a brilliant journey from the dark shadows of the self with its limitations and suffering.

FULFILMENT

Human consciousness is ever-evolving towards its origin of pure consciousness. To fulfil that natural drive we need to transcend our mental limitations by regular exercise of silence, stillness and to behave with modesty, kindness and accountability. The less we have outer ambitions, the more we are likely to awaken to our inner spiritual joy and wealth.

A child's desires and ambitions are endless and nothing is enough. Equally, for a spiritually-aspiring person no amount of insights and epiphanies are enough. As humans, we are in balance between breathing in, breathing out and other dualities. But our innate drive pushes us to go beyond balance, beyond boundaries and beyond all mental limitations. Moments of real happiness are rare but they do occur. When the mind is still and both body and heart are tranquil, inner joy fills the atmosphere with goodness and magic. You are just content and happy. So how did it all happen? You have gone beyond what you have desired and what you have hoped for. Now you are without needs or concerns. You are at one with your own soul. At that moment of happiness, you are not in any specific place or time, although you may associate the feeling of happiness with specific events and a place.

You discern light and knowledge through the shadow of darkness and ignorance. You aspire for well-being due to the experience of illness. Happiness will be experienced when misery is excluded. Put your lower self aside and the divine light in you is effulgent and fulfilling. You are in Na-Ku-Ja-Aabad, a place of bliss that is not a place. When you are truly happy you lose time and sense of yourself. To be durably fulfilled you need to access a zone in your own heart that doesn't belong to any place or time.

To experience life through the lens of your inner soul is to realise perfection in all situations. Initially you feel fulfilled once in a while but that's not good enough. You need to be sure that you access fulfilment perpetually. When you are in balance between body, mind and heart you hope to access fulfilment, irrespective of outer circumstances. You are obsessed with the desire for your own fulfilment and that means being at one with your own soul.

HEALTH AND WELL-BEING

The most primary drive in any living entity is to preserve life. My life is a spark that has emanated from cosmic life itself, and thus is the most valuable thing for me. Love for life leads to concern and desire for health and well-being. We love good health, painlessness and contentment. Our hopes, aspirations and activities assume a sustainable state of balance and well-being within body, mind and heart. This state of homeostasis is a precursor to transcending body, mind and heart.

We are at all times being stimulated and there is always a response. Our organs communicate with each other and share their state and condition at the physical, chemical and electrical levels. Billions of neurons connect all the different entities that constitute the personal universe of body, mind and heart. Our worldly experience is work in progress whilst we move toward higher consciousness. Physical problems are more urgent than mental and emotional ones. Then comes the most important need — spiritual awakening to our real identity, the soul within the heart. You have no option other than doing your best for yourself.

We are unaware of what is going on at the numerous levels of body, mind and heart. The human being is an intricate cosmic instrument that resonates at countless levels with visible and invisible entities and realities. What we perceive as normal consciousness is only one beam of many zones of consciousness. We are, in truth, like sleepwalkers pretending to be awake. We take it for granted that our body and mind function according to our wishes and expectations. We act without reference to higher consciousness, yet expect well-being and health as though it is something outside of us to be acquired. The doctor is expected to fix it.

Only when you accept being the custodian of your body, mind and heart, awareness of what you are doing will bring in natural balance. As an awakened being, a healthy body, mind and heart follow naturally. The ultimate criterion of well-being is the joy of being present in the moment. That is where body, mind and soul are at unison. The human part of you is within space-time, whilst your soul is fully plugged in with life that is perpetual and cosmic.

WAR AND RELIGION

After thousands of years of new experiences, discoveries of tools and the rise of human settlements, ideas regarding God and religion flourished and expanded. Shamans and Prophets accessed higher consciousness beyond the norm of cause and effect or reason. When the hunter-gatherers began their little settlements with horticulture and agriculture several thousand years ago, insights and revelations became guidelines for survival and peaceful coexistence in these small communities. The few so-called world religions encompassed practical issues for personal accountability, respect for others, as well as teachings regarding human nature, God and the hereafter. Without faith and acceptance of boundaries and trust in higher authority there will be destruction and chaos.

Religions helped consciousness to evolve beyond the immediate needs of cooperation, survival and livelihood. They brought about a higher reference that enabled common folk to accept and deal with the usual difficulties and challenges of everyday living. Religions and cultures often mix and merge together. Often what is considered religious is a cultural habit that may have its origin in a religious idea or dogma. Habits are important for ease of flow of life, whilst breaking habits helps with new openings and insights. Nowadays, most living religions and paths tend to accentuate the spiritual and transformative benefits.

Like everything else that expands and bifurcates with time, religions that brought about stability and bonding of people sometimes became the cause of destruction and warfare. Many wars have been waged in the name of religion, often under the banner that we are God's chosen people. How can anything exist unless it is part of the chosen package of creation?

The root cause of most wars is the inner war within the self, where the ego wishes to have the power and knowledge of the soul. The ego says "I would like to be in control and for everyone to obey me", while the soul laughs at the absurdity of this desire. Whereas war is conflict and disagreement, peace is love, harmony and unity, and as such will be the direction toward higher consciousness and the prevailing cosmic oneness.

Suffering And Suicide

All emotional, mental pain and suffering are due to the ego and the darkness it casts upon the soul. Suicide is a most drastic futile act, which attempts to put an end to this suffering. Instead of learning how to empty the cup, you break it.

Yet, every action contains within it an aspect of truth; fear, suffering and all aspects of misery are due to our self-ego which is given a spark of life from the soul and the perfect spirit. The rise of consciousness, and human evolution and the purpose of life on earth is to move by will from the lower darkness of the ever changing self to the eternal perfection of the soul. If that movement is not followed, then blame, claim and accusations increase fears and darkness leading to the point of utter despondency and the idea to end it all by suicide. It all began due to ignorance and can end up miserably due to lack of knowledge and direction. Many religions and enlightened beings have provided a path out of this darkness which can only be practical if it becomes a part of day-to-day life and culture.

The body is born to die. There is no birth without death, yet every balanced living being is driven to prolong life, honour life and consider it the most important gift in existence. So on what authority do you end a life whose nature and essence is unknown? Did you have any idea as to what life was when you were born?

Most world religions and spiritual paths aim towards transcending the ego and its love of self and to live as a soul. Ascending towards the higher level of consciousness may liberate you from tragedy and depression. The tendency of suicide is an expression of utter helplessness and lack of faith in the higher, which is why it is condemned by most religions and even by temporal law.

You cannot be durably content or happy until you live as a soul with the body and mind as temporary connectors to the outer world. So an awakened person may consider all human beings to be committing slow suicide in their day-to-day life. They are travelling towards death, yet they are not aware what perpetual life is. When personal life merges with cosmic life then you are living as a sacred cosmic soul that is eternal. If you carry on normal living without awakening to perpetual life itself, then surely you have not fulfilled the purpose of your journey on earth.

DEPRESSION AND CHEERFULNESS

There are different levels and types of depression — short term, chronic, mild or complicated. The state of depression affects one at all levels — physical, psychological and spiritual. Sorrow, fear and depression affect the move towards higher consciousness. Depression implies severance, disconnectedness, disappointment or loss of hope. Fear and sorrow are two major avenues, which can lead to chronic depression. The extent of fear and sorrow relates to the frequency and quality of the ability to transcend mind and its memory and values.

Life begins with a semipermeable membrane, with in-flow and out-flow. Harmony of flow is due to connectedness and balance between the outer and inner states. Most diseases are due to a blockage of flow of matter or energy. Difficulties, restrictions and barriers indicate lack of flow and appropriate connectedness. Lack of self-esteem can also cause blockages. There has to be a physical, mental and emotional flow and balance in an integrated way. These flows are necessary for the flow of celestial energy from the soul that keeps one alive. Life, as such, is not affected by the limitations of space-time, yet we only experience human life within space-time. Human life on earth becomes meaningful, fruitful and beautiful when personal life is consciously connected to eternal life itself. That pathway prescribes transcending conditioned consciousness to pure consciousness. Spiritual growth is based on accepting discernible limitations and then entering into complete stillness and silence, to be recharged by the soul's cosmic consciousness. The mental illusion of seeking freedom or liberation is a faint echo of the truth that the soul or spirit is ever-free and is not limited to any discernible factor.

If you are orientated towards higher consciousness and the presence of infinite reality, then you are in the spiritual flow where no fear, sorrow or depression has a place. Our higher spiritual nature is to be cheerful at all times, irrespective of the mental evaluation of a situation. Depression, sorrow and fears all belong to the shadowy world of ego-self and conditioned consciousness.

Honouring The Dead

It is an established human tradition to try and think well of a deceased person. People search for some past good deeds and encourage each other to think well of him or her. Why is this?

When we look at a dead body our memory takes us to the living being, and that relates to the soul. There is an innate regard for the soul as an echo of divine presence, and that is why we want to think only goodness. Reverence for graveyards and caution not to tread on dead bones is a reflection of respect for the unseen soul. The inner soul or spirit is like a holographic representation of God, ever-perfect, and perpetual. It is a celestial reality, energising terrestrial entities such as the body, mind and the illusion of independent identity.

The so-called "I" has a biography and identity that is constantly changing and updated. In essence we are the ever-living soul but for a short duration on earth we identify with the temporary material and mental realities of the body and mind. The most persistent driving force in this life is to go beyond the physical, biological limitations and boundaries. It is important to have a clear mind and wise judgment. It is more important to be able to leave that most important earthly asset aside and to experience the zone of the infinite reality and higher consciousness. Our conditioned consciousness drives us naturally to its origin. The truth is that life is perpetual and cosmic. Life is the only reality that is not subject to any change, and is our origin and destination.

To honour a dead person is an expression of remorse for the magic of life that was once vibrant in that body before it had parted. If you identify with the body, then there is only sorrow and misery. If you experience the soul, then it is alive forever and has just moved on beyond the material world. The body is material and is returning back to its earthly origin, while the soul is celestial and it is where it belongs, natural and perfect conclusions.

Suffering And Joy

As mind and personality develop, there is a natural tendency to rebel against restrictions or discipline. The adolescent does not want to accept any boundaries or conventions. The mind may follow its own fancy and illusions that lead to situations that cannot be reversed. It is part of human growth in consciousness to rebel and suffer. Regrets, fear and sorrow are all due to ignorance of the nature of reality and its dominance at all levels of consciousness.

When we become confused we suffer, as we are thrashed about by diverse sensations and conflicts generated by dualities, thoughts and memory. The first step out of suffering is to stop fear and be willing to accept outcomes that may not be desirable. You have to go through several stages in life until you have done a full circle; that is yoga. Struggle is the constant condition of mankind. You have to shed many skins. Our animal-self is necessary for our evolution in consciousness, and is also the cause of pain, anxiety, harmful emotions, anger, hatred and other tricks that we inflict upon our self and one another. Our lower self or ego is a necessary shield from the immense power of the soul early on in life, but becomes the obstacle in growth of consciousness. As a child, all that you have is the ego, as an adult it is your main stumbling block, and the cause of suffering and confusion. Misery can be reduced when you discover its cause and root — your own wayward self!

To trace the origin of suffering is the most important step in transcending it. When you consider that the suffering self will affect the body, mind and heart, and that the perfect soul is the origin and source of life, then you would like to refer your thoughts and desires to your soul and higher consciousness for sanction and approval. Through the occasional transcendence of your mind and identity, you touch higher consciousness that is sometimes referred to as conscience. In the rise of higher consciousness you enter another zone where joy can only increase with surrendering and abandonment of the lower self. You are much less significant than you even think, but within you lies the potential of experiencing the cosmic vastness of timelessness, where suffering becomes a distant past memory and joy prevails.

~

TRAGEDY AND LOSS

Human life is balanced between acceptance and rejection, highlighted by personal loss and gain. We remember tragedy, as well as happy moments. Pleasure and pain are inseparable. Highlighting pain or a tragedy is a warning of deviation and distraction, which ultimately lead to loss and regret. It is as though we wish to remind the self or ego, not to mislead us anymore. People stop on the side of the road to watch a terrible accident and others suffering. It is a warning not to speed up or sleep behind the steering wheel. Also, subconsciously by seeing that others are afflicted, we presume we have been spared. That is why gossip about other people's tragedies is prevalent and popular.

We all know how tricky the human self is, yet we need to give it some respect and attention otherwise we lose the sense of basic identity, human integrity and dignity. It is only with spiritual awakening and the knowledge that you are your own soul that any idea of self-image or dignity will vanish. The effect of sensing failure or loss is greater than its equivalent in success or gain. Why? Our focus seems to be more upon our mistakes and failures than goodness and gains. We generally tend to remember the occasions when we have made mistakes or endured life's rejections, taking for granted all the other acceptances and positive connections we have had. This wonderful gift of nature is to make us more aware of distraction and deviation from the real purpose of life, which is to be at one with the soul. That state is beyond any loss or gain. It is a quantum leap out of the box of limitations in space-time into the zone of the cosmic soul that encompasses the whole universe. We are frequently reminded of wasting time or opportunities to experience what is constant and real. The bias towards highlighting loss helps us to move in consciousness towards its origin and to awaken to god-consciousness of the soul itself.

If you celebrate outer success you must equally be prepared to weep for failures. These are inseparable twins, whose mother is pure consciousness. The rise in consciousness and the experience of the light of your own soul is that spiritual triumph, which is not subject to failure or success.

NATURALLY DISCONTENT

Our primary quest is for constant happiness or contentment, yet within space-time there is no reliable constancy. Once a desire or goal we are striving for is realised, our mind enters into a neutral state for a short while and we experience some contentment. But as soon as we are content, new factors arise and bring their own physical and mental challenges. So we are perpetually caught and trapped in the cage of change and uncertainties.

Human life is a constant struggle to move from discontentment towards contentment. But within every instant of contentment lies the root of the next discontentment. We love comfort and ease, yet know that it will be interspersed with discomfort and disease. We love the flow of pleasure, but also know that it is always tinged with pain. Even when we are satisfied and happy there is some hidden concern regarding the temporariness of that state. The nature of conditioned consciousness is based upon discontentment with occasional temporary contentment. The innate force within us drives us towards durable contentment and happiness, whilst our experiences are all the time subject to change and uncertainty. What we considered undesirable may turn out to be better that what we originally wanted.

Discontentment is a brilliant cause that moves us to discover a zone that is beyond the dualities of good and bad or attraction and repulsion. Only when we transcend our senses and mind can we touch higher consciousness, where all dualities vanish. Outer curtailments, limitations or loss can be the cause of frustration, disappointment, anger and even violence. Outer limitations can also lead to new openings and deeper insights towards durable inner contentment. We seek outer contentment as a starting point towards permanent inner contentment and joy of the soul.

Discontentment is an evolutionary force that drives us through numerous mental states towards a higher zone of consciousness, moving from the gross to the subtle. Once we experience well-being at body and mind, we seek subtler lights and delights of consciousness. We are terrestrial creatures seeking our celestial origin and reality. Discontentment will continue until the self yields completely to the soul and lives by its light, beyond any uncertainty or discontentment.

Remembrance And Forgetfulness

We would be overwhelmed if we were to remember everything, especially our mistakes, pain and sorrow. Forgetfulness is disconnectedness and remembrance is connectedness. The mind connects with what is needed and our thoughts focus on that. Equally it is good to forget mistakes and wrong intentions or actions. Deep within our soul lies the memory of its inception and life's origin and destiny. The soul connects with the essence of all knowledge, whereas the mind remembers, forgets and lives within the limitations of space-time.

The soul is cosmic and beyond definition and the mind's comprehension. Intelligence and sensory experiences are preliminary steps that may lead to transcendence to the zone of the timeless soul.

If there is a major question that faces us all the time it is a question of our original constant identity. The question reveals its own secret in that there is only eternal life. It is from there that the early stream of memory begins. It is such a powerful question that since we cannot answer it in the normal way, we seek distraction. We do everything to avoid facing this issue, and collectively deceive ourselves that we need a holiday or break from that which matters most. Collective amnesia enables the animal self to carry on. Individual human cleverness spawns collective stupidity.

Entertainment is easier than inner attainment. People tell each other: *"let's have fun!"*, and return to the same old miserable state, possibly even more incapacitated. Slowly we drift towards the most common malaise in today's world — depression. No wonder that we seek every kind of distraction with different levels of intensity and duration. The human mind is a master trickster and it wants to carry on without an end. Love for distraction is very deep in our psyche as we fear the end of life. We also fear the end of thought, or end of being usefully connected. As humans we like to forget about our wrong intentions and actions and to be reminded only of that which is in the direction of higher consciousness and durable goodness. We like to remember whatever increases our hope for a better quality of life with inner contentment and joy. We equally like to contain the lower tendency and the animal-self within us. We need to forget a lot and forgive a lot in order to be clean in mind and pure at heart. Then comes the intensity of the moment that has emanated from eternity and carries all the divine qualities of perfection. It is worth remembering this reality and forgetting all else.

REASON, RATIONALITY AND BEYOND

We consider reason and rationality as normal and desirable. Reason implies understanding, causality and other connectedness. Context and balance are also important in what we refer to as appropriateness or wisdom. We are all driven by accepting what we consider desirable and avoiding that which is not. The mind, however, is fused with emotional overtones that sometimes override conscious and rational efforts. The subconscious plays a big role in all intentions and actions. The most common concern of all human beings is that of death and the end of life, yet we postpone reflection upon this natural event. We live most of our time pursuing trivial day-to-day matters.

Much of our early human life is concerned with developing physical faculties, mental capacity and a smooth relationship between body, mind and heart. As earthly creatures much of our existence relates to physics, chemistry, biology and other natural energy streams. With maturity and middle age our interests and questions that go beyond the discernible and tangible gain importance. With old age many people may begin to consider issues that do not concern the younger generation, such as the nature and meaning of death and the experiences thereafter.

Think of human life as divided into three segments. The first is to do with basic growing up and maturing, the second relates to understanding and reflecting upon the forces that enable us to connect, continue and attain higher consciousness. The third stage is to focus more on the metaphysical or spiritual reality and the importance of the intangible part of our life which is unseen and beyond mind and reason. Many religions and spiritual paths define Reality as that which is permanent and never changes, while everything else including human life on earth are shadows that reflect this Reality.

Human experience is limited, changeable and will terminate with death. The soul which continues beyond space-time can be considered as real and as such beyond reason and rationality. The soul or spirit is a mysterious entity that carries the knowledge of whatever there is on heaven and earth. The full story is that we are both human and divine, temporary and permanent, all at the same time. We exercise reason and rationality within space-time as humans to the point of transcending our senses towards higher consciousness.

Perspective And Context

We are constantly trying to balance our dependence on others with our desire to be independent. Universal interdependence and self-governance contains countless pockets of localised dependencies. As part of our natural drive to be content and stable in our body, mind and heart we hope to be self-dependent or independent of outer forces. With religious and spiritual groups the notion of God-dependence is prevalent. Our natural love for power, longevity and dominance increases our drive to align ourselves with those who carry these qualities. Interest in magic and miracles may also exaggerate what we perceive to be supernatural. To be with God equals superiority over others. You get the news before others do. You know before others what He is up to now. If you know God's will or decrees, you are a carrier of divine secrets. With that haughty position, there naturally comes opposition, enmity and warfare.

Much of our well-being and contentment is dependent upon the extent of having higher and reliable perspectives. Personal points of view, prejudices and conditioned consciousness are basic to our humanity. These are foundations in our drive to go beyond the entrapment of space-time. We are all driven by our desire for wide, deep connectedness and continuity of life. We are obsessed with what is permanent, all-encompassing and ever present.

The art of alchemy was a process where a base metal would be helped to become gold by reducing the natural transition time of millions of years to a few years. Base human nature also needs to be transmuted to the divine nature that lies within. By reference to higher consciousness and putting everything in the appropriate perspective we are on the path to awakening to our real nature that is the source of all perspectives. The pure soul tells it all.

The foetus in the womb was not conscious of any of the difficulties that the growing child will experience. Our heritage is pure and perpetual life. This is the purpose and meaning of human life itself. The three C's: to connect, to continue and to grow in consciousness towards pure consciousness, are the drives in our life.

The Paranormal

Near death and out of body experiences, as well as what is considered paranormal, all indicate the limitations of the conditioned consciousness of the human mind. During an out of body experience, consciousness drifts out-of-body, mind and senses towards an intermediate zone without any signs to define or distinguish it. A most unusual experience that complements all that is labelled as normal. Altered states of consciousness and the paranormal relate to the experience of spiritual insight and awakening to a higher zone of consciousness, beyond shadows of ordinary dualities and mental constraints. Upon reflection the spiritual seeker will realise that all existence is experienced due to numerous zones of connectedness between lights, energies and matter. Darkness and shadows are only evidence of light and there are countless levels and qualities of lights.

The human body and mind is a temporary abode for the soul, which is liberated from those constraints by death. Due to our sensory perceptions and natural concern for survival, our priority is well-being and the connectedness and continuity of consciousness. The relentless drive towards discovery of the unknown, and the innate desire to understand death and reconcile with it makes us naturally curious about any strange phenomena that cannot be explained by the rational mind. The issue of normality and super-normality is like the relationship between matter and what is seen in the universe, with the vast unknown and unseen. Dark matter fills up 85% of what is in the universe. What is considered normal is miniscule in relationship to what exists and what affects our psyche.

An awakened being simply accepts the reality that much of what exists is beyond human understanding. What's wrong with that? Even on the human scale, it is such a blessing that we know very little of what is really going on. The secret lies in being in the moment and embracing its vastness without the burden of the past or fear of the future. We are accustomed to the flow of cause and effect and the laws of physics and other sciences but there are always exceptions to our expectations and some of these exceptions to the rule of normality can be labelled as miracles — beyond our understanding. The ultimate miracle of all times lies within the moment itself, and that is where both the normal and the paranormal meet.

CREATIVE DESTRUCTIVENESS

Every ambition or desire has an end goal. Truth has no end. As soon as a desire or ambition is fulfilled, new ones will arise. We always seek that which is better. Where is the end of goodness? What are we driving towards? An objective may be specific but soon leads to wider horizons, which ultimately cannot ever be fulfilled. All of this is the trick of the drive to higher consciousness.

The life of most people is a struggle to satisfy survival needs or to attend to ambitions and desires that are considered necessary or important. The drive for higher consciousness will reveal the connection between competition and cooperation. They merge into one when head and heart are in unison. With age and wisdom disappointments and failures will increase. That is why we feel the need to dampen the mind and distract ourselves from undesirable memories, hoping to attain sustainable contentment. Disappointment and suffering may lead to apathy, hedonism, a promising path or a religion, science or other diversions. The real solution is to give up the illusion of independence from cosmic light. To get rid of that illusion we require the artistry and courage of creative destructiveness. Fantasy is then replaced with Reality, the ever-present One.

Only few people live with the realisation that whatever is considered good or attractive has also within it the seeds of what is considered bad or repulsive. To understand the nature of the forces of life is to read the dynamics of dualities and most importantly the self-soul balance within us. A healthy spiritual seeker will desire what coincides with perfect destiny or the will of God — the drive to experience the perfect now.

The energy field of perfection and the real is accessible when you turn away from other fields of energy. The biggest issue in life is to make your will aligned with the cosmic flow, which includes all that is physical as well as metaphysical. To abandon human will to that which is manifesting from your own soul is what is referred to as salvation. This state does not exclude appropriate intentions and actions within the limitations of space-time.

When your physical state is in harmony with your mind and heart you experience life as an easy flow with delight, irrespective of outcome. The thrill of being completely in the present moment is superior to all other needs and desires. The highest and most persistent ambition is thereby fulfilled.

HIGHER CONSCIOUSNESS

Physical, mental and

higher awareness is part of

natural growth and evolvement.

For a child awareness relates to

what is immediate and sensory.

A mature person relates in

maintaining healthy conditions

at body, mind and heart levels.

There is a natural evolution in

consciousness leading towards

the higher level that is the state

of the soul itself.

ARC OF HUMAN CONSCIOUSNESS

Cosmic Spirit or Sacred Reality is the source of pure consciousness, and that is what we aspire for. It is the source of all life, power, knowledge and wealth beyond measure. Pure consciousness is a capacity and reality that has no colour or content, like pure water. It accepts whatever you put into it and reflects that. If fear enters my consciousness, then I will experience the world through the lens of fear. With love in my consciousness, then I see through the rose-tinted colour of love and unity. To put into perspective our diverse experiences, we need the calibration of pure and unconditioned consciousness. The more frequently we connect our experience with pure consciousness the more there is ease of flow and balance in our life.

Our earthly journey begins with basic baby awareness and grows towards full, awakened consciousness. The evolutionary process of consciousness becomes efficient and fast, if we are not blocked by the past or fearful about the future. To live fully in the now is to be at the meeting point between a specific describable consciousness and pure consciousness.

Conditioned human consciousness is to do with past experiences, the present moment and thoughts about future. The most potent and magical gift of time is the present moment. Now is the ever present messenger of timelessness.

Within the innermost of the present moment lies the spark of original singularity from which all time has emerged. Everything lies within this moment; the ultimate generosity in creation. The moment is like mounting Buraq or Pegasus, with a touch you are transported from mere existence to cosmic Presence, where effulgent manifestations encompass all that is seen and unseen.

The moment continues forever but no two moments are the same. Time lives and dies at the same time. The arc of consciousness spans beginnings and ends of human life: the first sentiency of the newly born and the last breath before death. It transcends body and mind. The soul continues its life towards its final destiny and return to origin.

BOOKS REFLECTING TRUTH

Humanity's relentless search for origin and purpose of creation gives rise to the idea of an original primal tablet that describes the secrets of existence. Religions rely on scriptures or the divine books of creation. Some of these sacred books promise that the divine secret and light is embedded within the human soul. The entire universe cannot contain the truth, but the heart of the awakened one can. Every human life tells a story whose essence is the same. Within this story, every aspect of existence is touched upon. There are galaxies, stars and countless infinitesimally-minute sub-particles. The universe and its beginning are a mirror image of the rise of human consciousness and self-awareness. Our physical bodies, with their intricate chemistry and nervous systems, in many ways reflect the birth, start and end of our universe.

This is a story worth telling and hearing. It can be understood if listened to by the spiritual ear, which functions when the other senses are switched off. This story reveals itself by itself clearly, when there are no interferences or distractions. It is supreme consciousness and cosmic light, which overflows by the grace of infinitude. This sacred primal tablet is of such power that it is revealed in steps and stages, so that our feeble, limited minds and bodies connect, understand it, then resonate with the soul and its divine origin.

Everyone in creation reads an aspect of the Book of Reality, but very few get the whole picture. Most of us are side-tracked and avoid what we consider to be beyond our control or grasp. Humans are natural creatures of space-time, and are bound by these limitations.

The Book describes patterns and designs that emerge from the infinite timelessness, which can only be accessed by total surrender and unison with that Reality when the mind and self are transcended. It is a revelation that is unique and can only be grasped when heart and soul are in the same sanctity of oneness. To experience this reality you need to refine and calibrate body, mind and heart, then transcend human consciousness to its original pure consciousness. All realities emanate from that zone, which is also called Truth and which is also described as being revealed in the Book.

DIVINE ATTRIBUTES

What is it that we all love and love the most and forever? Love and passion for life, power, ability, will, knowledge, to possess efficient sensory faculties through body and mind, and an illumined heart. These attributes are like fields of energy with specific qualities that help to lift consciousness towards subtler realms of consciousness. These key attributes are embedded within the soul, and are beamed towards the self, body and mind. If you enter fully into the consciousness of one of these attributes then you enter into the one next to it. Kindness is next to generosity and knowledge is with love. When you experience these states, you are close to essence and the vastness of the spectrum of consciousness. There lies the primal designs and effulgence of the unseen forces that govern this universe.

All of these fields emanate from oneness. As a separate entity or identity, you need to resonate with these attributes so that they lift you closer to their source. If you seek the knowledge and experience of higher consciousness, then embrace these qualities and climb the ladder of spiritual growth towards its origin. It is a great act of worship to reflect upon the divine attributes. The truth is that whatever there is in existence is glorifying, but this is not understood by most people! These names and attributes, like energy-beams, help to guide and lead us from earthly limitations towards the boundless realm of infinitude. We all struggle to climb out of the darkness of conditioned consciousness towards the lights of supreme Reality: Light of Lights. Embracing these attributes will curb the lower self and bring about greater awareness of conduct.

Ordinarily you are grappling with the mind and its ideas of what is a virtue and what is not. Transcending all senses is necessary for the journey to origin. From there on you enter the sanctum of Reality and Truth where all your previous climbing ladders and beams have led you. All your past is now like a faint dream. That is where there is only the divine light: Light of Lights.

When you step out of space-time then you are in the sacred zone of divine fulfilment and contentment — beyond all ambitions or needs.

Durable Fun

By simply mentioning to someone "let's have fun", you invite friendship. But what is fun? Can you have it without pain? And if so, for how long? And do you get it or does it get you? Again, for how long? Fun and games take us out of normal rationality and its limitations. A game has a beginning and an end, with some rules and pretence of it being real. Then it becomes a professional game, and with its seriousness comes also pain and sorrow. With series of monitors, accountants and cheerleaders, original fun is eroded. Serious competition and confrontation erode early cooperation and its fun. With so many rules and regulations, you need a team of trainers and lawyers to navigate you. Fun implies freedom and flow with ease. Many endeavours in life start creatively and enjoyably but soon new structures and regulations bring about fears and concerns. Once you plan and structure, concern for outcome and success erode the flow of fun.

The highest level of meditation and transcendence is when you lose all awareness of your senses and move from the usual conditioned consciousness and identity to a zone that is not restricted by space-time. There, fun is perpetual and endless. It is, in fact, sheer joy.

Earthly fun can also lead to disasters. Quite often young people's parties can end up with animosities and even violence. Even in weddings with hyped-up jollification you can detect subtle warfare with the fires of jealousies and other discord. If you are in the world of dualities then you cannot escape limitations and boundaries. To deny limitations you are denying the conditionality of earthly consciousness. Fun on earth, like all pleasures, is accompanied by some pain or fear.

Spiritual fun is another zone where good and bad have not yet separated from each other. It is joy and bliss, and not mere fun. Our earthly fun is a mere shadow of the joy within your own soul. We all yearn for that state, but stop short due to the interference of the animal ego self and fear of the unknown. What often begins as innocent discovery of connectedness can lead to differentiations, differences and discord. These are the three D's that will bring destruction and death. Reliable fun is spiritual drift in the land of timelessness without borders, perpetual fun.

THE GOOD LIFE

We naturally wish to feel well, content and cheerful. Life is all we have. We are totally dependent on it and our existence is drawn from it. The desire to be pleased with oneself is due to life celebrating itself with joy. I like to be pleased with myself because life is ever pleased with itself and since I am mostly familiar with myself I love myself. We love to love life. Beauty, harmony, well-being are expressions of a good life. The soul is ever in bliss and the self tries to reflect that reality. To be pleased with life is an experience of flow, harmony and goodness that are beamed from the all-encompassing cosmic oneness.

We try to avoid whatever is considered to be unlikely or unrealistic, as well as painful or negative emotions. Life on earth is transient. It is a mixture of what is considered good or bad, attractive or repulsive. It is a work in progress, to experience the ups and the downs, then by will and hope to transcend them all to higher consciousness, arriving through inner silence to where good and bad are not yet born. For good fortune and good luck, you need to banish the idea of misfortune or failures and success. Everything that we consider to be good reflects an aspect of goodness within our own soul and everything that is undesirable is a shadow of that light of goodness — experienced through the lower self or ego. When you interact with ease and grace in this world you don't deny limitations or the occasional setback. You are constantly nourished by the constancy of the Limitless. Even though personal life is balanced between birth and death, life itself is ever triumphant and beyond any change. The eternal life from which we draw our own personal life is ever perfect, ever complete and beyond all earthly values and limitations. The more you experience the infinitude of life within you, the less you have fears or sorrows. When you are pleased with life in a sustainable way you are recharged by higher consciousness from your own soul and feel more alive. The love for meditation, prayers and even wandering in nature can all be recharging to a limited degree. If you can be totally still in body, mind and heart, you are at the edge of perpetual life and the joy beyond pleasure and pain. A good life is the ultimate destiny we all seek. That blissful field of energy is ever there and to be within it you need to leave behind all other states. Good life beckons us all. Heavenly lights are our reality.

Dreams Within A Dream

Dreams are a re-ordering and housekeeping of what touches our mind and sensory faculties during wakeful periods — transitory states with no substantial reality. Isn't that also the case with our world when we are awake? Where is yesterday now? How often do you remember the tantrum you threw when three years old? Do you remember your mother's heartbeat in the womb? Collectively we deceive ourselves that our wakeful state is real. It may only be marginally more real than a dream.

Our senses help us to identify with our physical world by the imaginal faculty. It is this imaginal lens within us that creates the apparent physical realities of solidity, liquidity and other states and substances bestowing the illusion of separate durable reality. Without the restrictive ability of this faculty, we would bump into walls and sky dive from a mountaintop without fear and concern for personal survival. Conditioned consciousness is due to the imaginal faculty, which also enables us to ascend the ladder of creativity from limited consciousness up towards its origin of the cosmic soul from where all existential realities emerge. There are countless realities, starting with the most tangible and physical, and receding into movements of energies that are too subtle for us to measure.

We endeavour to be more awake, more alert, more knowledgeable and more enlightened. These words can be useful indicators, but more importantly, they mask the truth that we are talking about which is transitory, vague and can cause confusion. It is like a few people under the water near a shoreline, occasionally catching glimpses of the light and trees above. Some of them boast they are higher up than others but they are all under water. The majority of people are like sleepwalkers who appear to be purposeful. Everyone is convinced about the importance and goodness of what they are pursuing. Some of them are living a bad dream; others in a nightmare and many more are simply hallucinating. Almost everyone is sleep-walking to different degrees.

When you are honest and admit being caught within the cocoon of space-time, confused and lost, then suddenly the horizon of awakening will begin to appear. Confusion and suffering in the so-called real world may lead to openings and insights into higher reality. True certainty is the light of your own soul, a perpetual cosmic light.

LOVE OF OBLIVION

Most human activities point towards subtler realms of consciousness. Our creative activities which include much of art, music, and other sensory stimulations attempt to lift our consciousness to higher levels. We love to share experiences with others and the bond of sharing transcendental experiences is stronger than other bonds; yet we cannot share a most necessary experience, which is that of deep sleep. Quality sleep is an important component of well-being. To be relaxed, present and at ease implies accessing a wider range of consciousness than the intensity of focusing on one issue. It is fashionable to work hard and play hard. Our love for relaxation and recreation shows our pleasure when not pursuing an outcome or result. The process itself is what is enjoyed. Intense attention needs to be balanced by a drift in idleness and leisure. The desire to be relaxed and beyond thought is a natural drive and a prelude to higher consciousness and ultimately pure consciousness. Our destiny is that consciousness, with no content, and that is also our origin.

The prevalent fashion of alcohol and drugs that take you out of your mind are symptoms of our love to go beyond the mind. There is a hint of hope there if people start to realise we are not who we think we are and that all the illusions and fantasies and hopes we had have been part of our growing up. Most religious and spiritual paths prescribe practices that are often described as going beyond the conscious mind. That zone of consciousness is cosmic, which we in our conditioned state know of as oblivion. It is not oblivion that we love. We love that which is the origin and destiny of all.

We love boundlessness. We love timelessness. Love is the most powerful unifying field and it emanates from the original zone, which is not affected by creation and change. Absolute peace and stillness is a description of that zone, yet life can only be experienced with change and movement, which disturbs that peace and stillness. Your life is experienced through movement and it reaches its fulfilment when there is unison with cosmic life itself. Oblivion as such, is a departure from all sensory and mental experiences and a prelude to being in the zone of boundless consciousness: pure light.

Continuous Benefit

Every living creature is driven towards higher consciousness and to thereby benefit from a better state of life. Earthly life is a laboratory in which countless strands of energies and souls are learning the art of higher benefit and ultimately being at one with divine consciousness.

Everybody wants more benefit in quantity and equality. A child simply pursues whimsical self-interest, and immediate pleasure. A grown-up looks for benefits that are more valuable and durable. A wise person seeks benefits that may help others for the longest period of time. The natural drive of human consciousness is to benefit from the immediate environment, taking advantage of that relevant portion of time and place. Advantage refers to the motivation to achieve a better state in all life's experiences from the physical and material to the emotional and spiritual. The ultimate experience that we all seek to benefit from is the realisation of the presence of a field of energy that is self-perpetuating and ever perfect. A youngster takes advantage of his skills whenever he is in any contest or relationship. Short term matters most. A mature person acts with reflection on and reference to upon what is durably good. The desire to benefit and have an advantage follows numerous levels that include physical, mental and intellectual states. What we really seek is not a one-time success but perpetual victory, and that means a state that is not subject to any changes. It is this transcendental state that is above all measurable benefits.

The greatest and most durable benefit is to know that you are endowed with a treasure beyond any limitation, and that is your own soul. Once you realise the source of your own life then seeking outer benefits, and concern about the future, lose all importance. You are no longer distracted by changeable benefits. In this new state, there are no dualities, thus no idea of advantages or disadvantages. In the earthly zone of dualities, you are naturally competitive and driven towards being ahead of others. But once you enter unific consciousness and oneness, then you have gone past the struggles of multiplicities and dualities. You are now at the source, where there is only perfect divine goodness. Only perfect connectedness, perpetual life and cosmic consciousness prevail. The soul knows that divine state and transmits it.

Purposefulness And Destiny

Human life is held in balance between dualities and complementarities experienced as a swing between two experiences, what is desirable and what is not. We breathe in and out. We are awake or asleep. We are focused or distracted. Most of our efforts are to attain a steady state or a constancy of perspective and reference beyond this to-and-fro that encompasses wisdom at different levels. In our day-to-day purposefulness, we are like hamsters on a wheel and all our intentions and actions eventually lead to physical and mental exhaustion, culminating with complete stillness upon death. We love the occasional holiday idleness, where there is no mental drive to achieve anything. During occasions of quietude in body and mind we are at the connecting point of changing conditioned consciousness to ever-constant higher consciousness. If there is a persistent purpose in life, it is to realise the perpetuity of life itself and not the usual human madness of fluctuating between gladness and sadness celebrating new life or grief over death.

Human ability to control destiny is very limited, and the outcome is a state beyond predictions or expectations, especially regarding our emotional or spiritual state. Our objections and denials are due to ignorance or factors that were simply not initially considered. Wisdom is to move from denial and rejection to acceptance and connection with what is more pervasive and durable. Faith and trust in life's purpose is helpful during our transition back to sacred origin.

As an awakened being, you tap into the perpetual light of your own soul where origin and destiny are inseparable. What is perfect destiny other than origin itself? Perfect destiny is not a place or a time but a state from which all that appears emanates and returns to. The experience of your fate today is your temporary destiny. The final destiny is that all material and physical states end up with their origin — cosmic unity. Your body returns to the earthly elements from which it was collected and fashioned. The electromagnetic circuitry of your brain and mind will also return to the energy fields and elementary material states. Your destiny and your origin unite in the sacred zone from which all emanated from. Your final destiny is not separate from now! Space-time is a shadow that points to original infinitude.

THE DRIVE TO KNOW

Whatever we know and can share with others is within the confines of the world of dualities in space-time.

Whatever we know is a small sample of the vast ocean of knowledge that connects dualities with unity. The power of knowledge is due to the fact that it relates to cause and effect, beginnings and ends. Knowledge is a desirable major force emanating from oneness. We often respect people with higher intuitive sense who can foresee the future or the unseen. That is a natural drive towards higher consciousness and cosmic oneness.

Spiritual knowledge relates to what is beyond the boundary of space-time and points toward transcendence of the senses and submergence into the zone of timelessness. Religious and spiritually inclined people look for the unexpected and subtle connections between the seen and the unseen. We are heavenly creatures passing through earth. The human position is a link between physics and metaphysics. All our outer knowledge and wisdom is like a thin veneer upon the sacred ocean of original primal patterns and designs of every type of existence. What is unseen and unknown is much greater than whatever is discernible and knowable; like matter and energy, where tangible matter only constitutes a small portion relative to antimatter, dark matter and their subtler energy patterns. Limited earthly knowledge is only a small reflection of cosmic knowledge itself. Whatever we can know is only a metaphor for the boundless oceans of knowledge.

When you are content with what you know and what you do not know, you are at the door that connects human consciousness with its original cosmic light. What we know is within the confines of sensory appreciation and relates to cause and effect. That is a necessary balance for us to exercise as conscious human beings with responsibility to our intentions and actions. Carelessness may cause us pain and that it is not desirable. This knowledge helps us to preserve our life and drive towards higher consciousness. Our duty will be complete when we realise that life itself is perpetual and is not subject to the limitations of personal life. That celestial doorway takes us out of the realm of knowledge and ignorance into the celestial source and essence of knowledge.

TO AWAKEN

The human drive to
discover wider and deeper
knowledge leads towards
higher awakening.
Ultimate contentment and
happiness are by-products of
our connection with higher
consciousness without denying
the limited and conditioned
consciousness.
There are countless steps in this
awakening process. The ultimate
enlightenment is very similar to
its beginning of simple sentiency.

STABILITY AND UNCERTAINTY

We love safety and security, yet we also try to break boundaries and explore new worlds. Occasionally we are overwhelmed by the immensity of what is unknown. It is in human nature to desire power and the ability to bring about change. The ego of a child wants to dominate its immediate environment. The irony is that you seek to control in order to ensure your survival and dominance, while equally there is a hidden innate desire to be at the edge of a situation where you feel overwhelmed and helpless: such as the love to be overshadowed by great mountains, walk at the edge of a volcano or near an avalanche, or like a sailor face a mountain-like wave.

We love adventure and to push ourselves to the edge of possibilities and safety while still in control. Heroic acts or special breakthroughs often occur when the mind is transcended and conditioned consciousness is giving into the field of higher consciousness. For our humanity, it is healthy that we maintain limitations and accept that we have to work within them. Our spiritual thirst drives us out of the mental limitations for us to experience the vistas beyond the usual cause and effect, mental habits and limitations. Love has a reason that reason knows not.

We are intrinsically passionate about the infinite unseen, and are spiritually recharged by following the light of our own soul rather than the rationality and reason of the mind. Much of our day-to-day experiences in life relate to our need to balance head and heart or mind and soul. The love of distraction from the boredom of day-to-day activity and the tendency to gamble is to face uncertainty with the promise of sudden gain or wealth. Our physical and mental reality exists because it is energised by the cosmic treasure of the soul itself but that is not easy to realise. A child follows the whims of the self and ego. If a mature person does the same then distractions can only lead to destruction.

The whole universe is under perfect cosmic control through directional randomness. We are given a small degree of freedom to be in control within the small box of space-time. Yet all that exists follows cosmic patterns beyond what our feeble minds can comprehend. Only the heart and the soul can read this Truth and Reality.

Illusion Of Independence

It is human nature to want to be self-dependant and least in need of help or assistance from others. This innate drive reflects the soul's own perfect contentment and sufficiency. As the self evolves and begins to imagine its own independence, it learns to be deceptive and to deny that suffering and pain are due to the ignorance of the lower self. All injustices and disturbances emanate from self-delusion and give rise to separate or independent identity, thoughts and desires. With greater awakening and insight, we realise the advantage of honesty, transparency and admitting mistakes and errors.

A spiritually-minded person tries to use higher consciousness as a reference point to recalibrate directions and decisions. Ultimately, no one has real control on outcomes. What you desire intensely now could be the cause of deep suffering later. Many of our decisions will later be regretted, so how do we live with fewer regrets?

Full presence and awareness of our inner state and outer circumstances can reduce regrets and guilt. Everything is interdependent. Déjà vu and other similar experiences illustrate that your response to an event has already been decided in your gut and by millions of neurons other than those in the brain. The conscious or subconscious self is an aspect of this. The choice to have A or B has already been made before your mental comprehension and the illusion that you are deciding voluntarily. Your mind and your so-called personal choice simply confirm what has already been decided, which includes the conscious you and numerous other factors besides you. We desire the freedom to choose what suits us in our life as a natural outcome of feeling independent and self-responsible. The light and the force of responsibility emanate from the soul itself and if you can always take full responsibility then unison with soul is nearly complete. Through reflection and rationality, we can understand how complex interdependence is at all levels known and unknowable. With awakening to the light of the soul we experience the ultimate delight and contentment of trusting the perfect Reality that contains the whole universe and being at one with it. That state is beyond any ideas or thought of dependence, independence, duality or separation. Truth is One — Ever-Real and Ever-Present.

STUDENTS AND MASTERS

There are numerous types and levels of teachers who can provide maps and sketches that help in raising consciousness. Basic teachings relate to good conduct, courtesy, duty and accountability to others. Religious or spiritual teaching may help with wisdom, insights and openings towards higher consciousness. A fully awakened being may not be the best to teach others at lower levels of consciousness. Initially, you may listen to many, but as time goes on you listen to a few, until maybe you listen to only one, who may lead you to hear the voice of the One and only One in your own heart.

At the lower end of a ski slope many people can teach you how to stand up, slide or stop. At higher levels, there are fewer competent teachers. And at the peak, there are very few who have traversed dangerous grounds and unchartered territory. Earlier on, your needs are at basic physical and mental levels, learning correct manners and conduct. With maturity you need to find and follow a trusted teacher who can show you how to experience harmony and spiritual flow like an angelic dancer. Even a small mistake can be a serious setback at higher levels of consciousness. Once you have excelled in being in that state of flow and harmony, then the grace of the Master of the Universe is your teacher. Your own soul in your heart is His agent!

The relevance and the appropriateness of the teaching and its effect is more important than the personality of a teacher. Perfect teaching will put an end to the illusion that there is any reality other than the cosmic source and its universal presence and manifestations. In truth, there is one Master, and that mastery pervades the whole universe and acts at all levels. The best teacher reflects your own inner state and its degree of wholesomeness and its relationship to the outer world. Context and the right perspective are essential references to be in the harmonious flow of the moment. The ultimate purpose of all teaching and knowledge is to live in the now so completely that you lose your lower self and its confinement within space-time. The good earthly teacher reveals that truth and acts as a mirror that reflects for you the lights of cosmic Reality. Anything else can be misleading or a distraction.

SILENCE

It is healthy to encourage a child to express his or her self and even better to help the child to reflect the meaning and purpose of their expressions. A mature person in contrast often considers the overall situation and connections before speaking. Calibration with a higher level of consciousness makes speech and communication appropriate and optimum. Who are you talking to? What are you saying? Why is it the right time to say that? How are you saying it?

Language is due to the mysterious medium of sound vibrations, letters, words and symbols. It can enhance good connections and bonding but it can also cause misunderstanding, disagreement and even destruction. Without sound vibrations you cannot imagine quarrels or wars. When emotions and feelings, especially anger, fear and disappointment, accompany speech communication, it becomes tarnished with other energy fields that can bring about unexpected outcomes. If anybody feels threatened or accused of wrong-doing there is an immediate protective state that impairs the connections. Disharmony and enmity flourish on blames, claims, denials, threats and fears.

Our universe is interconnected and sound vibrations are an important stimulation and response for the human species. The effect of sound and sensory stimulation takes place at physical, chemical, biological, electromagnetic and other energy levels. Due to this complex energy interaction we need to listen carefully beyond the sound of words, in order to get the full message and nuances. Regular and frequent, long and short periods of silence will enhance the state of our consciousness and improve the potency and appropriateness of speech and communication. During silence, spiritual energy from your soul can recharge your mind and other faculties and improve your efficiency to connect and understand. All communications are means to relate appropriately to what may be dispersed and separate. The entire universe was within singularity before it manifested as creation. We seek efficiency and connectedness in communication as an attempt to raise consciousness towards original oneness.

The Pilgrim

The friends of the Sufi sage were enquiring about his journey and where he was going and for how long. One of them said, *"all of us want to see the kingdom of God on earth and the true Jerusalem."* Another wise man said, *"every one of us wants to go back home but where is it?"* The desire to discover the perfect home, the perfect family and perfect time is deep in the psyche of everyone.

Before going on pilgrimage, the sage spent a week in prayers, reflection and meditation, which culminated in a farewell gathering. There he was asked, *"How can I be ready to visit the sacred precinct? Do I have Allah's blessing?"* The sage said, *"All of existence is afloat upon God's blessing but the illusion of separation creates the fantasy of independence, personal will and freedom to act. Place and time are the earthly veils that accompany God's light. Your confused identity asks the question. Transcend your body and mind and you may touch upon the reality of sacred Presence here, there and everywhere, and at all times—from before time to beyond the end of time."*

A pilgrim to-be then pleaded, *"Should I not make effort and struggle towards Him?"* The sage answered, *"that is necessary for beginners. When the Truth engulfs you, the idea of effort will delay the realisation of the Truth: an illusion fearing its conclusion. There is One — the Real. You will know and experience it when all shadows and ideas of otherness vanish. You got used to yourself, therefore you prolong or delay ascending to life's purpose and direction to be at infinitude. It is normal to become accustomed to confusion and darkness. In many cases the familiar is a hindrance to growth in consciousness and the natural evolvement from self to soul or earth to heaven. There is only the light of the truth declaring the Real. When the illusion of otherness vanishes, there is only the perfect soul reflecting the sacred precinct and cosmos: the Kaaba of Truth. All else are phantom illusions. Wherever you are, the Real is there already. There is only Him. There is only One. You too are also one. He is the One that is incomparable, but you are one like the others in essence, whilst different in appearance and biography. Your worldly life has a beginning and an end, and in between you struggle, seek, attempt to understand and know. Within you lies the essence of cosmic oneness, and that is your soul's secret."*

Transcending Fear And Sorrow

Suffering due to fear or sorrow relates to unfulfilled desires, disappointments, illusions, confusions and distractions from soul consciousness. An intelligent seeker desires to live without fear, sorrow, regrets, or anything that is undesirable or detrimental to awakening. It is common wisdom to advise people how to avoid persistent sorrow or grief. It is equally fashionable to help people to be more courageous and have no fear. Positive thinking has become a commonly-accepted desirable trait even though it is an illusion and out of balance. We are naturally driven towards a higher zone of consciousness where fear, sorrow and most other emotions weaken and are replaced by good expectations and presence at mind and heart. Pure consciousness sheds light upon all earthly shadows and darkness.

Our natural drive towards awakening will save us from much fear and sorrow that can only be transcended when perpetual life of the soul is realised and known. What is the purpose of fear or sorrow to begin with? Is it redundant as far as the human project is concerned? Like the ego, when fear and sorrow are fully transcended, it will be realised how important it was to have them. The natural drive to reduce pain or sorrow relates to our relentless concern to preserve life and its continuity. Fear or grief can be incentives to transcend these emotions towards an awakening to cosmic life.

With fear and sorrow you are miserable, without them you are still discontent because contentment lies in the higher and spiritual zone of consciousness that is not confined to your mind and humanity. There is always fear and sorrow until you awaken to a state beyond your body, mind and sensory realities. Instead of fighting fear and sorrow — and their closest companion, desire — it can be more effective to acknowledge them and transcend the mind that created them. Then, you are at the shore of perfect Reality. That state is a paradigm shift. Sheer contentment and joy is a divine grace and is ever there, but you are not there because your mind and thoughts occupy you and drive you along what you erroneously perceive as happiness. Cosmic consciousness is the origin and destination. This source of life radiates from your own soul, which exudes bliss and joy.

Shaykh Fadhlalla Haeri

BELIEF AND NON-BELIEF

It is human nature to believe and trust. Hope is the belief that tomorrow may be better than today.

Crisis of faith and belief is natural to many human beings. Truth, Reality or God's existence are sometimes reinforced by denial. Everything that exists is within the cosmic governance of the Real. A big challenge in today's world is to justify religious beliefs and connect them with modern ideas and scientific discoveries. Religious dogmas have also often been used to increase conflicts and violence.

Most thoughts begin with some doubt. There cannot be any certainty without some doubt in it. Throughout human history the idea of God as the All-Powerful, Omnipotent, the Controller of the universe and other attributes has spread out throughout humanity. The past few thousand years have seen theological packages and religions defining God with a few nuances and cultural modifications. It is natural for the baby to adore the mother as a source of nourishment and light that provides comfort and contentment. From there on we always look for what provides wellness and happiness for us. With some reflection we can calculate that there is a universal source that produces all these needs and emotions. Most of our ideas of religion and God are mental constructs with Truth as the origin. We are driven to believe and have trust and faith in a higher power or light that permeates the universe and leads it to its destiny. The human soul by its innate nature is fully attuned to its origin. The soul's light radiates to the body and mind and produces the idea of belief, faith and trust. We love to trust and believe in something that is all-powerful, generous, just and durable. Living faith helps to transcend the senses and to be at one with higher consciousness. This state is greater than any belief, faith or description. You will simply experience the cosmic truth of absolute oneness.

Reality, Truth or God are not understandable by our feeble mind and rationality. If you accept the concept that Reality is the cause and the essence of all that exists known and unknown, then at least you have a usable concept or sketch of that which is beyond us but is our origin and source of life and power. You will never know God by mind or reason but every knowledge is like a beam of light that emanates from God. In truth there is only God and what emanates from that source is beyond normal, mental doubt, belief or confusion.

LIFE AS A METAPHOR FOR REALITY

Every living entity is obsessed with life and wants to enhance its quality and continuity. Love for power is a reminder of the presence of the All-Powerful. The high regard given for patience is a metaphor for infinite patience or timelessness. Reality is not subject to patience or impatience. It is ever there and constant.

Desirable qualities and so-called virtues are all helpful along the path of rising in consciousness. Generosity and treating others as you wish to be treated widens the vistas of connectedness to other beings. The more we see ourselves in others, the less we are concerned or fearful of otherness or obsessed with our own selves.

When you begin to see the light of the soul of other people you are connecting limited conditioned consciousness with the prevailing higher consciousness. We like peace, ease, harmony and contentment. All of these and other desirable states enable us to be less controlled by our mind and illusions of identity. When the mind is quiet and there is contentment for the moment, the light of your soul enables you to experience a touch of the infinite presence. Eventually a state may arise that you don't experience your life as your own, but simply as a reflection of or resonance with eternal life itself. It is useful to remember that physical birth from the mother's womb is the first stage to experience spiritual birth and the ascent from lower consciousness to supreme consciousness.

Our life on earth is a work in progress to realise the original divine perfection that pervades the universe, which includes what we consider to be chaos or imperfect. Whatever you desire to achieve in this world and whatever you hope to avoid are indicators of the nature of life after death. If you have done your work to ascend to the highest level of lights, then you zoom past paradise. Otherwise there is a continuing process that takes place after death that is referred to in religions as purgatory or the purification of the soul from earthly impurities.

For the fully awakened being there is little concern for either hell or paradise in the hereafter. He or she has repeatedly experienced attraction and repulsion and the constant desire for perpetual joy that has been discovered to be the natural quality and state of the soul and its unity with its origin and essence.

Questions And Answers

The nature of the human mind is to explore the unknown and overcome problems that may prevent a pleasant flow in life. We always seek comfort and ease so that the mind is still and quiet, until the next challenge arises. Life has its perfect patterns, and everyone desires smooth flow in day-to-day living. We want answers so that the mind relaxes and we experience tranquillity and ease. It is by asking questions that we open the door for the answer to come in. The answers are all there, like beams of light and the questions are only their shadows. The question begs the answer, and the answer is waiting to be unified with the question and to be invited by the question which indicates readiness to receive the answer.

We are naturally full of questions and constantly looking for satisfying answers. As consciousness evolves the nature of questions and answers change, until a point is reached where you are sufficiently tuned to the inner heart. You will then find your question is an excuse for the answer to appear. The answer is what had sent the question? We don't see it that way because we are used to the arrow of time. When you are ready for the answer, your question ushers the answer. For the awakened being there are no questions or answers. There is Reality and Truth itself, perpetually everywhere and at all times.

Conditioned consciousness and its evolution is the cosmic trick to reveal the utter oneness of all that is seen as differentiated realities. That is how we are tricked to be led along what we describe as rich experiences or a good life. There is no good or bad life; it is only the extent of ignorance and veil of dualities that shields us from life's perfections. When you move from conditioned consciousness and its ever-changing content to pure consciousness, that original essence of sacred energy has no questions or answers within it, yet the whole universe emerges from it. This great miracle is before all questions and answers. So, stop asking! Trust and experience the joy of the moment.

Live in the moment. Trust in the perfection of Reality. Now you are at the door of awakening to perpetual life.

∽

SPACE — TIME AND BEYOND

All human experiences take place within space-time. This is the biggest challenge to all human endeavours, especially science. Our life is a series of experiences with a beginning and end, the cycle of which repeats itself over and over again. Even a child always asks about the end. On a journey everybody wonders when it will end. When a story-teller drags on, the audience will be agitated, wanting to know the end. All is well that ends well. All is well at all times and every situation, if only you can read it well in relation to timelessness.

Human life is a drive towards exploration and discovery but where will this stop? When curiosity stops or ends. Impatience is generally regarded as a handicap, yet within it lies the ultimate wisdom of the desire to know the end of time. We decry wasting time and we recommend saving time but these notions will vanish whenever you touch upon the zone of timelessness.

There are generally two practices that may help us touch upon the experience of timelessness. One is to go faster than time or faster than light where mass comes to nothing and what we consider as normal on earthly life will end or stop time by transcending all sensory consciousness. The human mind can go faster than light and can stop time. The light of the sun reaches the earth after eight minutes. Your imagination can take you to the sun and back in one second!

Most people seem to be short of time except for the awakened one who has all the time because of his or her experience of timelessness. Patience is ultimately slowing of time or stopping it. Our desire for a quiet mind drives us to expect that our wishes are fulfilled instantly right here and now. For this reason we value speed of delivery and efficiency in achieving anything that makes the mind content. Whatever can make you content immediately here and now will be popular and profitable. We long to be free of desires and needs because that state is the prelude to transcending all sensory experiences and earthly constraints.

The spiritual seeker hopes to discover that now is the best time ever and that everyone is wasting their time until they directly experience timelessness. That is the most auspicious time. You are at one with the grace that has emanated from the zone beyond any time or space.

STAGES OF AWAKENING

Life's experience flows along the upward arc towards higher consciousness. Our waking up from sleep is a metaphor of a step towards awakening to higher reality and cosmic consciousness. When you first wake up from deep sleep you connect with your senses, your hearing, your sight, your touch, then connect and correlate things into perspective. Your mind is now fully alert and you are aware of the place, time and what is it you are going to do. Your normal day-to-day state enables you to accumulate experiences that may lead you to better understanding of the world around you so you function more efficiently. It is the same thing with spiritual awakening. The more you relate to higher consciousness, the easier it is to put things in perspective and have less concern about emotional entanglement, fear and sorrow. What is required is a commitment and passion towards higher consciousness. Persistence, trust and stillness in body and mind are needed at all times. You persist until you are exhausted. You may even weep, and wish to give up and die. Now you are at the door of cosmic consciousness. Here one needs to be relaxed and at ease to transcend the normal state of basic awareness. We constantly experience stillness and movement, the easier and quicker we can switch between these two modes the healthier is our mental state and awareness. It is only by grace and divine mercy that you may experience the infinitude of Reality and full awakening. A good life implies continuous rise in consciousness until one accesses pure consciousness constantly.

Spiritual seekers have a tendency to discuss the levels of enlightenment or awakening. Aspiration towards awakening may be accompanied by measurements and comparisons. What you can discuss and share is the extent of leaving behind fears, sorrows, anxieties, desires and other natural human concerns. You cannot understand by language and the limitations of the mind a zone of consciousness that is boundless. It is a wise seeker who has trust and flows with transcendence rather than be anxious or concerned about stages of awakening. Everyone will awaken to truth after death, so what is the rush? To move away from what causes misery and avoid egotistic pitfalls and distractions is a healthy path. The anxiety about awakening is an illicit endeavour. Trust and persistence will naturally lead to great awakening.

NEEDING NOTHING

A baby does not know its needs but acts according to its autonomic state. Soon, the consciousness of separation and identity drives the youngster to discover and ask how things connect so as to satisfy the ever-increasing desires and needs. The wise, mature person tries to curb frivolous needs and attachments. We all seek freedom or liberation from one need or another, yet no one can be devoid of needs, hopes or attachments.

An attachment to an idea or a thing is simply due to a mental or emotional link that can be reduced or severed if replaced by a different one. A desire for a definable material or physical entity is easier to satisfy than subtler feelings, or emotions. Where an attachment to something or someone is definable it can cause less fear or sorrow than when it is subtle and emotional. The comfort of a warm room in winter is easier to attain than acquiring status and respect from others.

We are naturally attracted to what our senses and mind consider attractive. Let the physical attraction become mental and the mental, spiritual. If the attachment is not to a beautiful thing only but to beauty itself, then the item takes one to a sublime state of higher understanding.

The idea of freedom never dies, even when people are in a pleasant, safe, just and humane environment. Once you are free from hunger, pain, political or economic injustice, you will be looking for other ideas or states of freedom. There are two zones of freedom. The one is within the personal human-conditioned consciousness, such as to rise above material and mental limitations, for example to be free from pain. The other is freedom from the limitations of culture, religion and other issues.

You cannot get out of this existence, but you can dive into its core and essence. That essence is beyond all limitations. Your own soul is boundless. The human soul has no needs and is totally connected with the cosmic soul — God.

Our deep drive to go beyond needs simply means to go beyond conditioned consciousness, where there are no fears, attachments, needs or desires.

AWAKENING TO COSMIC CONSCIOUSNESS

Where is Truth and how can it be attained? Where is Reality or God and how can It or S/He be reached? Such questions are endless; the drive towards the answers can be diverse and often do not lead to a reliable conclusion.

The fact that we all search for enlightenment or God's light implies that there is within us a deep subconscious notion of the original light from where all subsidiary lights or existences emerge. The essence that brings about the experience of birth or death is what is desired by all, and that desire will always be fulfilled with death when barriers and filters of body and mind are lost. The consciousness of all living creatures begins at birth and grows to a point of peak personal conditioned consciousness. Then, it subsides with age and ends with pure consciousness from where it began.

People who are on a spiritual quest are driven to know truth and try to imitate someone alive or dead who they think has attained truth. Quite frequently they become confused and much suffering comes from the attempt of imitating someone else. Concern and anxiety to wake up can be a big barrier towards a quality life and awakening itself. Progress is nothing more than being in constant reference to higher or pure consciousness. Most spiritual practices try to calm the mind so that one transcends all the senses to that zone of pure consciousness. Living the moment fully brings about deep contentment and trust in the ever-present perfection. This experience is more rewarding than the usual struggles and other spiritual drives towards the idea of awakening or enlightenment.

If you wake up to the now and live in the moment you have done what can be done, to be between human consciousness that is changing, and its origin and sustainer, pure consciousness. Enlightenment and awakening are states or fields of energies that are everywhere, but it is you and I that need to leave behind other concerns and be exclusive to that sacred field which is sometimes referred to as paradise. We are programmed to aspire and drive to experience that perfect state. That state is within the soul that resides in your heart. If you exclude all else, and tap into the light of your own soul then you are illumined by what is called the light of enlightenment.

REALITY

Our humanity is not

separate from cosmic divinity.

It emanates from it and leads to it.

Reality or Truth is cosmic

and perpetual.

All other experiences are

illumined by the Source.

MEASURES WITHIN THE IMMEASURABLE

There are times that some of us wish to withdraw from the normal working day challenges in life. Temples, monasteries and other religious institutions, especially in the past, enabled a few people to pass through life without the usual worldly pressures and demands. In today's world, spiritual pursuits may be considered as unusual and a seeker may be accused of being a drop-out. Our desire to evaluate, measure and rationalise a situation is a natural exercise in the earthly nursery of evolving consciousness. All moves towards higher consciousness must take into account our human and physical state and needs. Truth and Reality are immeasurable but we all connect mostly with each other through the measurable.

A child needs to learn reason and rationality, but a wise person regards most rational and human values as temporary as child's play without denying their relative importance. When the measurable leads to the infinite realm of the immeasurable, the light of higher consciousness illumines all realities and perspectives. Truth and Reality are beyond measure.

Whatever we evaluate and measure is within the confinement of space-time, which is dependent on boundlessness itself. The digital world and its high dependence upon the mysterious quantum realities can be very helpful to connect the visible world with the invisible. Birds navigate by familiarity with topographical signs using trees, hills or buildings as signposts. But when they migrate, they switch off this local map and read the earth's electromagnetic field to navigate thousands of kilometres of flight. The vastness of the electromagnetic field and the countless types of radiations and energies demonstrate the immensity of what emerges from the original cosmic light.

Transient life is based on reason, rationality and other values, all of which will vanish in the vast zone of higher consciousness and the immeasurable beyond. Personal life is like the drop of rain that is on its way back to the ocean. The measurable contains the secret of the immeasurable. The awakened being evaluates rationally what is discernible, then takes reference from beyond and acts in a manner that is not always understandable by common folk.

Sacred Space

In some places, it is easier to connect with higher levels of emotions, feelings, insights and spiritual openings than other places. We like these uplifting experiences. We like to create places where we experience higher levels of connectedness, helped by prayers and meditation to rise above the mundane and the limited. We feel refreshed and energised by higher consciousness. The idea of sacred space is deep within the human psyche, and is beamed by the soul which is one's own personal sacred space.

To enter a sacred place you need to leave your mind behind, reduce and stop your sensory connections. A successful pilgrimage is when you transcend all your thoughts, past identities and values. We are both earthly and heavenly, and spiritual progress relates to focusing more upon our spiritual reality without fully ignoring our physical side. When you constantly recalibrate with infinite silence then everything else is noise. It is by taking yourself out of yourself that you experience sacredness. We all aspire to transcend the limitations of our minds and bodies because our life is dependent on the energy transmitted from our own soul, which is cosmic and celestial, giving life to the terrestrial realm. Your soul presents you with an identity that you yearn for at all times and in all situations. Your limitations and need for sleep or conscious meditation are attempts to go past ordinary consciousness. We are all obsessed with the desire to experience boundlessness and timelessness.

Physics and metaphysics unite at source and destiny. Discernible existence is a shadow of cosmic Reality and reflects much of its innate qualities. We need to recalibrate with the sacred within it. No doubt that the positioning of these sacred spaces relates to ley lines and other energy forces that appear on earth, as well as, of course, the energies that accumulate in and around them due to human traces such as supplications, chanting, hopes and yearning. Every living entity occupies some space, and because of the life within it, we can consider that space as sacred. The whole universe emanates from the sacred effulgence of the Divine.

LOVE, PASSION AND OBSESSION

Love is the universal unifying force in existence that is experienced in numerous ways and intensities. Being tolerant of someone is at the lower end of empathy and human connectedness. Higher on the scale is to like someone, to love, adore and ultimately to be passionate about. High intensity of passion is akin to burning with a yearning that can lead to an obsessive attachment. At that state, object and subject merge in a state of oneness — for a while. With love you lose self-concern and normal rational consideration. With passionate obsession you lose yourself and any sense of separation and identity.

Obsession is at the foundation of higher consciousness. It can also be a distraction that may end with emotional confusion and a degree of madness. Essentially, we are obsessed with perpetual reality, which is the quality of our own soul. The tendency for addiction is a natural human drive as our origin is singularity and oneness. We are always propelled towards that which is permanent and not subject to change. To be prone to addiction reveals our innate and natural addiction to a Reality that is the source of all that appears and disappears. Everyone is addicted to soul and spirit. Everyone loves one's own self and your self is only there because of your soul. In truth, every living creature is passionately obsessed with its own soul. That realisation is the ultimate liberation from all illusions and confusions.

Human beings are naturally creatures of love and passion. The dark side of that is hatred, anger and disappointment. Our conditioned consciousness spans dualities at all times. Good is always accompanied by the seeds of bad. There is no beauty without ugliness or success without failure. The drive of passion is to go beyond the confusion of duality and to be at one with cosmic unity or god consciousness.

Obsession is the pull of original oneness and is also driven to oneness due to the experience of separation. Human desires, attachments and obsessions are drives towards unity. The desire to love, to be passionate and obsessed is rooted in the original unity and singularity from which creation and existence manifested. Love is the facilitator of experiencing unity and oneness that emanate from the original source. The experience of love brings closeness and ends distance and absence, a great invitation to all-encompassing Oneness, the ultimate generosity!

Boundless And Eternal

Every one of us is both local and universal. You sometimes experience life as a trap, prison or even a torture chamber. Sometimes you may also experience life as glorious, beautiful and utterly joyful. The human journey is based upon countless links, connections and interdependencies at physical, chemical, mental and other levels with other creations and the universe at large. Durable bond is through higher consciousness and spiritual reality with its perpetual perfection. We are limited within our physical framework and mental capacity, while the nature of our soul is cosmic and boundless. That is the reason for everyone's yearning to experience boundlessness.

Our terrestrial exposure carries with it the challenges and limitations of dualities, whilst aspiring to experience the perfection of unity of the soul within. The struggle to get out of the box of limitations can lead you to realise that in truth you are your own soul. The self tries to take on the quality of the soul, which is its source of life. The soul provides the energy and life and the self is its companion shadow until death. To be enlightened by the soul you need to extinguish the self. To obtain the essence and perfume of a rose it must be crushed for it to lose its physical identity so that it reveals the subtle essence of its perfume. A lump of coal will radiate light and heat when it is ignited. So the self too can be illumined when awakened to its real nature as a soul or it can remain dull and confined to its egotistic darkness. To be enlightened the self must give up its identity and merge with reality of its soul. Appropriate intentions, attention and action enhance the authenticity of the drive towards higher consciousness and soul awareness. The mind needs to experience its intention, to be convinced that you are making effort and progress towards a desirable end. What is that end? And if it is real, then it is not subject to space-time. That end is already here and has always been present.

The illusion of going through barriers and stages in life encourages the human side in us to keep on driving towards higher consciousness. Healthy illusions may lead to a supreme conclusion. Otherwise you end up mixed-up in depressing confusion. The soul is the essential nature of the human being and it reflects the cosmic Reality of boundlessness and timelessness.

RELIGIOUS PATH AND FAITH

The essential innate drive of religious ideas and paths is to connect visible human condition with transcendental realities, which encompass the past, present and future. We are all driven to know that which is constant, permanent and ever-present. Religions appear to satisfy the needs of a particular time and place, then end up becoming cultural, organised and structured. When the ideas of religion become rigid, terrestrial and earthly without constant reference to the divine essence, the likelihood of violence, sectarianism and war become real.

When the sage was about to leave the city somebody at the gate asked him, *"Don't you like our city? We have everything here."* The sage replied, *"I don't see people striving for perfect destiny or celebrating divine Presence and without that direction people will be confused and chaos will prevail as a natural prelude for renewal."*

Awakened people often see through what appears to be pleasant and acceptable, and remind us that the inner state is camouflaged by outer appearances. Outward strength and security of a people is often balanced by inner weakness and vulnerability.

The innate aggression in most of us manifests in unexpected ways, and when curbed, produces other ailments and even new diseases. If you are on a path towards awakening, then anything you witness on your way can be a helpful sign or indicator. That state requires sensitivity to both mind and heart. The mind may object to a discipline but the heart reads it as needed to improve on attention, focus and clarity of direction. However, if your own path is not clear, you are not completely committed to it and trust it, you may fall into traps and distractions all the time. In this world of dualities it is necessary to be on a narrow and defined path to arrive at unity.

Peace is an energy field that is always there and we can only enter it through complete silence and stillness in body and mind. The perfect beauty and majesty of peace is obscured by movements and change within space-time. The origin of existence is perfect peace and so is its end. That state is ever-present. Religions and spiritual paths attempt to describe helpful maps in order for the seekers of truth to attain oneness with Truth.

RELIANCE ON GOD

It is natural to seek knowledge, power, ability and other desirable qualities. If you consider these qualities are godly then it is natural that you want to be close to God. We all desire to be considered special. This is most pronounced with children. The soul within is super special. Where the danger lies is that many people think that they are special with exclusive access to God. This belief brings about an aspect of superiority. With that attitude comes the idea that others should revere you and you actually begin to believe your elevated status and try to enhance that profile. Many people wish to be God's agent so when the establishment helps them to qualify through priesthood or other ways, you have spiritual materialism. If the main quality of God is perfect justice, then how can anybody be excluded from the divine Power that sustains all?

You start by relying on the mother, then other members of the family and friends, and that circle then expands to others. With spiritual orientation and meditation, you will benefit from God consciousness. Constant reliance on God will pave the way to a perfect outcome and not necessarily as you had expected. God's wisdom is beyond us.

The idea of trust and reliance on God takes our consciousness to the highest point of reference. That idea can never fail. The danger lies in flaunting this concept and using it to diminish other people's spiritual potential and to inflate one's spiritual power to the exclusion of others. That pretence can bring about higher status and material advantages. It is easy to make money using religious power, irrespective of how real or false it is.

Now that you accept the notion of relying on God, what is the extent of your reliance on God? If your project goes wrong, are you still in utter gratitude to God? Or do you cry "Oh God, why have you forsaken me?" An omnipotent God cannot forsake anything because whatever exists emanates from that source and is sustained by it. It is your idea of a personalised, local and domesticated God that brings in the doubt. True reliance on God will take you to a state where you know at all times that there is only God the Doer, and if you have been acting then that is only by proxy and permission. In reality, power is exclusive to God. The soul is God's agent on earth and the human project is to realise this clear direct link and dependence on God.

THE BIGGEST QUESTION

Human position is in the middle between the infinitely big and the infinitely small. We are in awe of big mountains, great rivers, the gushing volcano and anything that is awesome or bigger than normal. Where is the biggest? Where is the biggest idea? Where is the biggest news? Where is the biggest treasure? What is the biggest danger to a happy life?

For the spiritual seeker the biggest question is to know the real self and be at one with the soul. The biggest question begs the biggest answer. You are alive because of your soul that is like a holographic representation of cosmic life itself, both of which are hidden. Your real purpose of life is to rise in consciousness to awaken to the magnificent truth. There is only cosmic oneness — eternally.

For those who are concerned with spiritual awakening, they may consider the biggest question to be how to get the self out of itself. If you are truly immersed in the biggest question, then the real answer will show itself.

Being in the present moment continuously is to be in touch with infinity and timelessness beyond space-time. In religious language this may be called unison with the will of God. Human life and its progress are towards this state. We all have desires and hopes that often lead us to regrets and disappointments. When your intention and action are outflows of unconditional love with no concern for the outcome or acknowledgement, then it is unlikely to cause you harm, sorrow or regret. The Will of God is to know that there is only God and whatever is God's Will will prevail, so you need to be subservient to the divine Will.

The mind can accept this reality if it reflects deeply upon the multitude of factors that bring about the present moment. Most of these factors are not in your hands, so all you can do is to clarify your outer intention and attention and act as best as you can. If the outcome is durably good and is appreciated, that is a bonus. If not, you have done your best and traces of sorrow and regret will just slip by. The big challenge is how to utilise the energy you have been given to act within space-time so that you don't regret it, or accuse others of being inadequate. Be at one with the One and there will be no fear or sorrow due to otherness. That may be the end of all serious questions. What remains is the perfect moment.

THE HOLY FOOL

Reason and rationality are considered as normal and necessary for life's progress. There is generally a consensus for what is considered a desirable and acceptable norm and what is not. The mind, however, is very tricky with the hidden forces of the subconscious and ever-changing circumstances with needs, emotions, and feelings that often override the conscious or rational. The deepest fear and concern of all human beings is that of death. It is also the most postponed or ignored, as it is not an issue that can be resolved by cursory reflection or discourse. That may be the part of the subconscious that declares life in itself is perpetual, even though one's personal life will go through the paradigm shift of death.

We find in some cultures that a court jester would say things to the king that other mortals did not dare to. Holy fools appear with different names and personalities in most stories of the past, and because they are not taken seriously they could say what others would not. Often people remember and quote some utterances of a holy fool because of the deep meaning of the saying, even though the person was considered eccentric or abnormal.

Most people are caught within their conditioned consciousness and fear exposure to other unfamiliar horizons or places of consciousness. The holy fool jokingly sheds a beam of light on ordinary viewpoints that needed to be reviewed and given fresh, new consideration.

To be god-obsessed or intoxicated by the dazzling lights of singularity will render what is considered normal or have value, absurd and stupid. The wise fool is occasionally valued as a safety valve to release pent-up confusion or anger due to fear or habitual politeness. God's ways are most complex and beyond the human mind to comprehend.

The holy fool is a tolerated outsider until his utterances become too painful or dangerous with regard to conventional ways. We enjoy changes and challenges until they begin to question the foundation of our culture, belief or common conventions. When the core of our apparent stability is questioned, we are alarmed, act with fear and even violence. Truth finds its way in strange ways and often in unexpected times and places.

FULL ACCOUNTABILITY

Without a reliable reference or perspective, mistakes and distractions lead us to darkness and loss. To begin with, we are unaware of the need for self-correction and acceptance of outer boundaries but with wisdom and the desire for liberation, we realise the necessity of accepting limitations and accountability at all times. The relationship between a child and a mother is based on love, trust, affection and empathy, which are the roots of accountability. The healthy child fears rejection and that fear can lead to honesty, transparency and accountability.

With time and experience, the mature person is unlikely to embark on action unless the consequences are imagined and faced. Accountability implies deeper reflection regarding one's interaction with other people or situations. The lower self is harnessed and led by the inner light through accountability. Ultimate destiny is that place of constant light of the perfect soul within.

If you are completely self-aware and live in the moment, then there is very little concern about the hereafter, purgatory, hell and paradise.

You can accept, even welcome, death and be at peace with this inevitable event when you know that it leads to perpetual life and a higher plane of consciousness. There are numerous versions of death experiences that begin with deep sleep or a coma. With physical death, the soul separates from the body, mind, energy and matter, and enters into another cycle of re-emergence. Death is not the end of life. It is the beginning of celestial consciousness after the turbulent earthly duality, experiences and challenges. It is final liberation for the awakened being and a shock for others due to the experience of loss of personal power or will.

If your personal life has led you to cosmic life itself, then it is a beautiful natural transfer of consciousness. If your personal life is at one with cosmic life, then death marks the glorious beginning of a liberated spirit.

THE SAGE HAS LESS

Spiritual materialism is rampant. The love for power drives us to the illusion of being more powerful than others. If only you can get God to do what you want. This God is only an invention of a sick and disturbed mind. If you can fully stop your mind, you may catch a glimpse of the infinite truth. There is only God and not the one you imagined. There is only Reality pervading the entire cosmos, and every other reality carries a spark of the Real. There will only be cosmic chaos if the God of people's imagination listens and answers every caller. Can you imagine the outcome of every supplication being answered? What a horrendous and maxi-moronic world it would be.

Most people try to improve on their lives whilst carrying increasing baggage, physically, mentally and emotionally. The successful person on the path of awakening sheds this baggage as much as possible. When outwardly you have less than others, you may have the capacity of having more inwardly. In truth, your soul cannot have more than what it already has. It is a cosmic treasure. Once you discover the inner map, then you can enjoy the journey of consciousness and realise life's immense richness. We normally enjoy acquiring objects and ideas during our life's journey. A time may come that you find most of what you have collected is inconsequential for living in the moment. To be present in the now, you need to be less burdened by the past and less concerned about the future. The wider and deeper your connection to the outer world, the less is the intensity of the experience of the present moment.

A spiritual journey may start with uncertainty and be fuelled by the hope of reducing outer dependencies and needs. The sage takes from this world what is really needed for an illumined life. He has less of the burden than others carry. Intelligent people often long for a simple, quality life, but end up encumbered by belongings, attachments and desires. Cheerful awareness of death may be a remedy for being under the weight of what is considered important. The awakened being has realised the truth of the cosmic soul as being the only reality and as such nobody owns or controls that reality. Freedom from possessions and obsessions are natural steps towards being at one with cosmic governance and controls beyond all limitations.

TAKE YOUR TIME

Flow with grace. Take your time, and then hurry. There is urgency in time for you to experience timelessness. Your body and mind are trapped in it anyway. Take all the time you need because it has possessed you. You cannot stop trying to catch time, nor can you stop the conclusion that it has caught you. To know the meaning of time is the biggest challenge in human life. The human mind and its physical base of brain and neurons, enables the senses to process and experience past, present and future, making the human story appear continuous and durable. We value time, and even say "time is money" or "don't waste time". This love affair with time is a reflection of the passion for the perpetual soul. The natural human concern for losing time or that time may be up reflects the spiritual responsibility to awaken to the timelessness of the soul. The urge to have more time is the drive towards discovery of the eternal soul.

The key towards awakening is to transcend all sensory experiences and that state is beyond space-time. When you experience your soul, space-time will lose its significance.

The sage said, *"I feel well, content, without fears, sorrows or desires. I am blissfully present in an intoxicating moment connecting now with eternity, connected by grace and bliss. This is a good time to leave everything else behind and return to the origin. A good point to leave the moment. For all the same reasons, it is a good time to stay. After all, our efforts and hopes are to experience the best of times. Here it is. So, it is the right time to hold onto the moment and stay where the past, present and future meet."*

This is the space of Truth. The door towards higher consciousness is via total presence in the now and absence from everything else. Time is past, present, future and none of them. The now is at the event horizon where it vanishes into nothingness and is perpetually recreated as another now. Initially you touch upon the now and then miss it, until such time there is only now without the illusion of moving time. What a magnificent love affair!

DIVINE PRESENCE

Sacred light permeates existence, ever-constant as Truth and the Real, but remains elusive to us due to the activity of the mind and our separate personal identities. To experience full presence, you have to die from other-than-it and be at one in this endless ocean. When there is any otherness or thoughts in the mind, a struggle and striving takes place and acts as a filter for the sacred light.

A seeker had sacrificed what he loved and experienced the beauty and gratification of selfless acts, yet, he was not fully content. The sacred voice whispered, "*It is I who is the cause of his dissatisfaction and discontentment. It is I who has given value to virtues and repulsion to vices. All of it is emanating from Me. Now he should stop trying and enter the divine precinct. Stop everything and die into oneness and live by it forever.*" The Prophet taught "die before you die". Leave the illusory self to its original light, the perpetual soul. Be at one with Presence and forget all you experienced whilst in the cocoon of space-time.

Wakefulness or presence has many stages. A corpse may be present. So is the one in a coma. When you first awaken from sleep, you have some presence, but that is not the same as when you are fully conscious and alert. Most of our wakeful experiences in life are vague and sometimes confused. Due to our cultural and personal values, needs and preferences, we only witness situations and events partially. Our love for life and survival causes us to judge, discriminate and desire all the time. The mind discerns and chooses all the time, but to whose advantage? What is the conclusion of your hopes and wishes? Most of what you witness is already coloured by your past prejudices. Most of us most of the time are only partially present, so how can we discuss divine presence, which implies cosmic perfection, utter beauty and majesty? Humanity drives us towards our divine origin all the time. We are in constant struggle and try to climb the ladder of presence to the sacred precinct of cosmic perfection. That presence is a Reality without definable identity. When the self is completely given up to the soul, and the soul's light illumines body, mind and heart, then therein lies divine Presence, and that is the source of life and boundless joy. We are driven to that state by its own original source of cosmic Presence.

BEYOND AWAKENING!

Ambition and drive towards discoveries and fulfilments are natural human characteristics. The range is very wide, culminating in boundlessness. Through meditation or psychotropic drugs many people experience boundless consciousness or a touch of infinitude. Religious people often refer to it in religious terms, with a certain amount of reverential confusion, as sacredness, divine precinct, holy spot or bliss. There is usually an insinuation that a teacher, master or guru (dead or alive) can give it to you. The gullibility of humans is such that we really do think that someway, somehow, somebody can take you out of the misery of yourself.

The gift of life within everyone is like a well that continuously provides quality water and sustenance. With the growth of conditioned consciousness and our minds, habits and accumulated memories, this well gets filled up with debris and junk that only you know the extent and density of it. For quality life, you have to clear out the junk from your well. Nobody else can do it for you. Because of your natural self-absorption and self-concern, you may not know clearly what obstacles and barriers you have acquired. So, the help of someone else as an indicator or mirror may be needed. At best, you need a friend or a person with empathy or love to simply remind you. No one can actually heal you except yourself. Your self is only there because of your soul and your soul resonates with God. So, it is God's help and connection you need, and it may appear as a human being or an inner voice, vision or inspiration.

The full spectrum of human consciousness spans the limitations within space-time, as well as cosmic consciousness. An enlightened person accesses this entire spectrum of consciousness but will not deny human limitations. Thus, the awakened being is at ease and content with all the absurdities of humanity due to constant awareness of supreme Reality and its perfection at all levels.

Shaykh Fadhlalla Haeri

THERE IT IS

All dualities point to their
original unity.
The biological birth is only half
the story. The other side of the
coin is spiritual awakening and
realisation of the eternal truth,
rather than the transitory
personal awareness with all its
fears and sorrows.
The purpose of human life is
to acknowledge limitations,
changes and movements in time
with constant reference to that
which is ever perpetual, often
referred to as God.

THERE IT IS

Most human beings go through life with ever-increasing questions, challenges and desires to know, succeed and be content. The intelligent being hopes to do the appropriate thing in the right way at the right time. The wise one is always concerned more about giving than taking. The seeker of truth will try to serve others with least expectation. An awakened being knows that there is one Reality from which every soul derives its life force and therefore in truth all human beings are the same at heart. It is only outer differences of body and mind that separate people.

The underlying forces that govern the universe are interlinked and reinforce themselves. Everything emanates from unity and manifests as dualities and pluralities. Energy and matter are ever-interlinked. The good and the bad are inseparable. Self and soul are the foundations of human nature. Your soul is a replica of cosmic life, while your self is a shadow of it. Your life's journey on earth is to link them together so that the light of your soul leads. The individual and communal life is also a significant example of the interplay of dualities. What the others think, and their past habits, constitute the social fabric and gives rise to numerous challenges and puzzles as culture and memes. Sometimes sudden changes in behaviour and conduct may occur that is not based on rationality or reason. Group dynamics obliterate the individual's so-called normal behaviour. Whatever we do or intend falls within the forces of the three C's which is to *Connect* and that includes the love to belong, to *Continue* which is the love for eternal life, and to be at the highest level of *Consciousness*. No living entity escapes these fundamental forces.

When you realise that the cosmic soul governs the universe, then whatever was considered personally important becomes less significant. The soul knows its origin and destination, and beams unconditional love and life. Divine mercy and grace are the ultimate gift that permeates all that is known and unknown. Your soul is your master and the elusive self is its shadow that exists as its earthly companion and connector to physical realities. This ego-self is proof of the soul's life-force and leads to it. In truth, there is only the Divine Spirit; there is only Truth and whatever exists carries a spark of that Truth and points to it.

No two minutes are the same, no two beings are the same, and no two events are ever the same. Yet what each one of us desires and hopes for is reliability, predictability, certainty, freedom from pain, fear and sorrow. Every human being desires the experience of love, security, contentment and happiness. In what is important we are all the same, in what is not important we are different.

The origin of life may coincide with what we consider to be the origin of creation or the earth itself. This mystery reveals itself in glimpses. In a deep meditative state, we may drift into a zone of timelessness beyond normal consciousness. That is perhaps as close as we human beings can get to the source and sacred origin.

The awakened person knows that in truth there is only the timeless presence of the One Real. As far as spiritual awakening is concerned most human beings are like children. You may repeatedly remind them that the purpose of life is to awaken to the vastness and eternal nature of life itself rather than prolonging human life or pursuing temporary pleasures and fleeting happiness. If you know this truth you have no option other than sharing it, even though most people will not give it the urgency it deserves and just carry on with their old habits of identifying themselves with their body, mind and social habits, rather than the quest for spiritual reality. Life on earth follows a rising arc of consciousness, connecting physics with metaphysics. The little that is observable and tangible is ever-connected with the vastness of that which is unknown and boundless.

If you are fully present in the moment then no fear or sorrow can affect you. You will only witness the events as moving forms and energies, with some empathy and connection with them. Everything that exists is according to patterns and designs that will lead to an on-going drift of uncertainty except for its overall direction back to origin. Every living creature is a celestial, timeless reality journeying through a terrestrial realm, with cycles after cycles and constant change that gives the illusion of events which lead to hope or despair. Existence and life is self-organising and will change and adjust following a destiny of perfect efficiency and ease of flow.

The big news is that whatever we think of, intend or act upon will have its impact upon our life positively or negatively. To rise higher in consciousness we need to discard our past thoughts, habits, fears, concerns, guilt and remorse. We need a fresh and clear mind, least encumbered with prejudices and old values. Then the pure heart will beam the light of the soul to reveal local and higher realities for what they are.

Human consciousness spans the mind's reason and rationality, and the soul's light and insights. We are used to the habit of being boxed within space-time and conditioned consciousness, yet we are always looking for ways of freedom and liberation from earthly limitations. We need a clear mind and a pure heart to access higher consciousness and the light of our own soul or spirit, which is in control. Without acknowledging our humanity, empathy and sympathy with others we are in denial of the earthly manifestation of spirituality.

For a seeker of truth and the meaning and purpose of life, it is necessary to accept humanity, its limitations and aspirations by maintaining a constant reference to life, its essence and divine origin. You are born into this world from your mother's womb, now it is your duty towards your self to awaken to the real you that is your own soul within your heart. Nobody can give you the ultimate gift of the divine treasure of being one with your own soul except yourself by constant effort to transcend sensory limitations and through divine grace. Your first need is to get yourself out of the morass and confusion of earthly dualities and mental confusion.

Whatever we experience is within duality and emanates from unity. Energy is not separate from matter. Nor is life from death. When body and mind are in a healthy state, the light of the heart can lead toward the best of selfless actions energised by unconditional love: all of which emanate from the soul. The most beautiful fragrant rose has emerged from stinking compost. Each one of us can also emerge from our confused darkness of ignorance to the cosmic light that holds the entire universe within its perfect grace. Each one of us needs to be engaged with situations that can reduce the natural egotistical tendencies and perhaps lead us to experience the presence of divine generosity. When you have awakened to this knowledge, then you are truly alive physically, mentally and spiritually. Before that you have to pierce through several layers of veils and barriers that you have acquired due to your daily interactions and relationships, which have given you your earthly illusion of personal identity.

Most human beings and some other living creatures have the apparent choice to act and experience the outcome of their actions. Many ancient cultures had numerous gods or lords for different activities. The God of Safety on ocean passage is different to the God of Fertility. In the Abrahamic and Islamic traditions, there are numerous attributes of Allah that can act as guidelines in your endeavours. Sometimes you need to be fast and other times slow and patient. You invoke different attributes for different needs. Our earthly life is like being in a gymnasium where we act, interact or be still to catch glimpses of perfections and their numerous fields of energy. By our own desires and actions we are on the ladder of consciousness towards its origin of pure consciousness. Our earthly life is the practice and experience of different stages of harmony in order to attain momentary perfections, contentment and happiness. These experiences can lead to the realisation that the whole universe is governed by perfect grace, and our worldly journey is preparing us for full encounter with this grace after death. If you are fortunate enough to witness divine perfection and presence then you have no fear of death. You are then as content and happy as anyone can be. You are awakened to your own soul which is God's agent within you.

Whatever you want to attain in a material sense or intellectually, you need to follow the pattern that may lead to the desired outcome. Whatever exists connects along the arrow of time that you cannot reverse. Without knowledge, good intentions can end up in disaster. Whatever you are doing is part of a process that has a beginning and an end. Enter the house through its intended entrance or you may fall through a window and face the consequences. Appropriate and timely knowledge is a great gift and source of power. Earthly wisdom is a prelude to heavenly insights and delights.

Our experience and evaluation of the outer world are according to our inner state. If you are well, content and happy, you will see much goodness and harmony around you. If you are hungry, in pain or grief, you see misery and trouble. Every moment is a balance between the outer world and your inner. To maintain a healthy equilibrium and balance you need to review your personal evaluation and judgment of a situation and then move on to read the situation as a clear and honest witness. We are all prejudiced and we cannot survive without it but with the accumulation of our likes and dislikes we become judgmental and will be veiled from the reality behind the event we judge. For spiritual growth and expansion of consciousness, accept your judgment, but leave your evaluation and emotions behind. Then, you may witness the event for what it is and read other messages that it carries. Recognise your bias, and then leave it for higher reality. Gifts are all around us but our minds are preoccupied and we miss them. We are often like sleepwalkers on the edge of disaster.

Divine grace encompasses everything that exists, and durable progress for humanity is to understand and experience this truth, irrespective of personal expectations or needs. To move up the ladder of higher consciousness you need to leave lower, conditioned consciousness. For you to be embraced by cosmic love you need to leave behind fears and hate. For you to grow spiritually towards awakening you need to be ever-vigilant regarding the shadowy ego and animal self. Like a zookeeper you need to feed the animal so it can at least experience survival, then lock it up gently but firmly in your inner zoo. The higher self or soul is the light that illumines all these shadows and casts its brightness way beyond.

The ultimate mystery is the soul or spirit that carries traces and knowledge of all there is in the universe. Every one of us is a cosmic being exposed to countless permutations of connections between matter and energy, form and meaning. Your life's journey is like a walk in a sacred park, where every grass and flower and tree has its own story and cycle of beginnings and ends. Your human side also has a beginning and an end. Its existence is due to the divine light within you and that is who you really are. When you live this truth, fears and sorrows will become insignificant. You have little self-concern and your care for creation assumes a higher level of understanding and effectiveness. Love and affection becomes transformative.

We are most fortunate to be living in this time and age. Humanity has evolved greatly in consciousness, whereas in the past a few illumined beings existed amidst the emerging masses. No doubt there are still many serious and dangerous black spots in today's life that show our vulnerability and even the risk of extinction of life on earth, but on the positive side, information and knowledge is accessible to almost all, which was not the case in the past.

In this book, I tried to share with you that within your heart is a light that knows the whole story before it began and after it ends. Also to share with you that as humans we are all caught within the limitations of conditioned consciousness. We have no option other than to accept outer limitations and practice the connection with higher consciousness. Occasionally we may be thrilled to experience the connection between the seen and the unseen, and how fate prevails. We are in this world but not confined to it. Peak human consciousness is only a reflection of the cosmic consciousness that is our origin and destiny. Our duty and purpose is to make our thoughts and actions subservient to our spiritual reality and its light. When this state of awakening or enlightenment is established then you are reconciled with the earthly limitations and the veils of body, mind and thoughts that connects the soul with the outer world. These limitations will fall away upon death and the separation of the soul from its earthly encumbrances. This process is described as purgatory and the experience of punishment or reward, hell or paradise. Death is the celebration of the soul and its liberation from its temporary limited confinement. Truth is victorious and divine lights are ever-alive and effulgent. We need to discover the map that will guide us to awakening to this timeless Truth.

Political problems, economic insecurity and environmental crisis are all due to deep darkness and ignorance of the basic nature and purpose of humanity. If it doesn't rise towards its cosmic reality it will simply whither and vanish into its cosmic black hole. We have evolved considerably in our sciences but we remain infants with regard to accessing higher consciousness. Form and meaning are inseparable, the same as energy and matter, so are personal life and perpetual life.

Human life evolves from within the womb of space-time, and consciousness drives every one of us towards the experience of what is beyond space-time. Our beginning and our end are inseparable.

To be born into the infinitude of cosmic oneness your midwife is your own soul, and the umbilical cord to be cut is the illusion of separation and duality.

OVERVIEW

The most natural human drive is to investigate and know the physical, emotional and other aspects of life. From babyhood onward we are stimulated to connect cause and effect and learn how to avoid what is undesirable and attract what is desirable. At the physical, psychological and mental levels we are balanced between attraction and repulsion, give and take, input and output, sleep and action. We are interconnected at numerous levels of discernible, as well as unknown forces.

At all times in our wakeful state we desire well-being and balance within our body, mind and heart. Physical and mental well-being naturally lead to higher states of consciousness and spiritual insights. Human nature is both earthly and heavenly, while our love for beauty, harmony and the fragrance of a garden are like the earthly nursery that may lead us towards the discovery of the inner heavenly garden — the sacred soul within, eternally perfect.

The natural drive to be stable, secure and happy are preludes to experiencing a higher consciousness, which is beyond anything that is discernible. The feeling of bliss, euphoria and joy touches our consciousness due to transcendence of mind and senses. A clear mind and healthy body are needed for basic earthly activities and survival. It is necessary to go beyond them to touch the inner spirit or soul. Important earthly needs can never be completely satisfied as we are obsessed with a state that is beyond fulfilment, which can occur when we transcend the zone of earthly consciousness. Lose yourself in an earthly garden and you may be at the gates of its heavenly origin.

Human consciousness is affected by numerous levels of stimuli and responses. The human microcosm mirrors the vast macrocosm. We want to know and experience everything on earth and beyond. We are heavenly spirits in earthly transit. Our origin and spirit are beyond space-time and so contain everything that is temporary and constant. Most reflective people occasionally experience being trapped and caught within the limited boundaries of earthly existence. Lasting relief can occur when one awakens to the truth that in reality one is a soul, thus beyond the limits of space or time. We are briefly trapped in our earthly bodies and will experience relief through direct experience of the light of the soul within.

The most crucial human duty or responsibility is to know the nature of the self and be in constant awareness and reference to the permanent soul or spirit within.

All human experiences and conditioned earthly consciousness are experienced in dualities and pluralities — light can be discerned due to darkness, good and bad are inseparable. Earthly wisdom implies understanding and acting appropriately within space -time, which is relative and changeable. Higher consciousness and awakening leads to transcendence of all limitations. Body and mind are rooted in earth, while the soul within the heart is heavenly.

The origin of the word "educate" in Latin is both "educere" which means to bring out that which is hidden and "educare", to train or to mould. The ultimate knowledge and experience is to witness the earthly garden as a metaphor for the heavenly one. The love of beauty, harmony and peace is the unconditional love of divine grace and its spiritual agents. The garden and its meaning are our nursery on earth.

The Garden Of Meaning